THE BOOK OF
A LA CARTE
RECIPES

THE BOOK OF
A LA CARTE
RECIPES

a Salamander book

Published by Salamander Books Limited
LONDON ● NEW YORK

Published by Salamander Books Ltd
129-137 York Way, London N7 9LG, United Kingdom

© Salamander Books Ltd., 1991

Recipes and photographs on the following pages
are the copyright of Merehurst Press,
and credited as follows:
18, 19, 20, 21, 22, 23, 29, 52, 53, 54, 55, 56, 57, 58, 59, 60, 61,
62, 63, 64, 65, 71, 72, 73, 74, 75, 76, 77, 93, 94, 95

ISBN 0 86101 626 2

Distributed by Hodder & Stoughton Services, P.O. Box 6,
Mill Road, Dunton Green, Sevenoaks, Kent TN13 2XX

CREDITS

Designer: Sara Cooper

Contributing authors: June Budgen, Linda Fraser,
Kerenza Harries, Lesley Mackley, Janice Murfitt, Mary Norwak,
Lorna Rhodes, Sally Taylor, Steven Wheeler

Typeset by: Maron Graphics Ltd., Wembley

Colour separation by: Fotographics Ltd., J. Film Process Ltd.,
Kentscan Ltd,. Magnum Graphics Ltd., Scantrans Pte. Ltd.

Photographers: Simon Butcher, Per Ericson, David Gill,
Paul Grater, Alan Newnham, Jon Stewart, Alister Thorpe

Printed in Italy

CONTENTS

Soups
pages 7-17

Appetizers
pages 18-27

Fish and Seafood
pages 28-34

Meat, Poultry and Game Dishes
pages 35-51

Crêpes and Omelettes
pages 52-65

Salads
pages 66-70

Fondues
pages 71-77

Desserts and Cakes
pages 78-95

Index
page 96

PROVENÇAL FISH CHOWDER

NEW ENGLAND CLAM CHOWDER

60 ml (2 fl oz/¼ cup) virgin olive oil
1 small onion, finely chopped
1 leek, trimmed and finely sliced
2 cloves garlic, crushed
375 g (12 oz) ripe tomatoes, skinned and diced
bouquet garni
1 bay leaf
250 g (8 oz) potatoes, diced
1.5 litres (2½ pints/6 cups) fish stock
3 teaspoons tomato purée (paste)
750 g (1½ lb) white fish, such as cod, skinned and
    boned
½ teaspoon dried basil
60 g (2 oz) small black olives, stoned and halved
salt and pepper

two 315 g (10 oz) cans clams
90 g (3 oz) back bacon, rinded and diced
1 onion, finely chopped
500 g (1 lb) potatoes, diced
315 ml (10 fl oz/1¼ cups) fish stock
315 ml (10 fl oz/1¼ cups) milk
155 ml (5 fl oz/⅔ cup) single (light) cream
pinch dried thyme
salt and pepper
fresh thyme leaves or paprika to garnish

Drain clams, reserving liquid, then chop and
set aside.

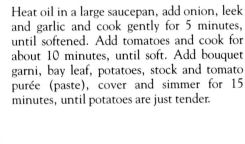

Heat oil in a large saucepan, add onion, leek
and garlic and cook gently for 5 minutes,
until softened. Add tomatoes and cook for
about 10 minutes, until soft. Add bouquet
garni, bay leaf, potatoes, stock and tomato
purée (paste), cover and simmer for 15
minutes, until potatoes are just tender.

Put bacon into a saucepan and fry over high
heat until fat runs and bacon is lightly
browned. Add onion and cook until soft,
then add potatoes, liquid from clams, fish
stock and milk. Bring to the boil, then cover
and simmer for about 20 minutes, or until
potatoes are tender.

Cut fish into 4 cm (1½ in) pieces and add to
soup with basil and olives. Season, then
remove bouquet garni and bay leaf before
serving.

Serves 4-6.

Stir in cream, clams, thyme and salt and
pepper, then reheat for a few minutes: do not
boil. Serve garnished with thyme or paprika.

Serves 6.

SHRIMP BISQUE

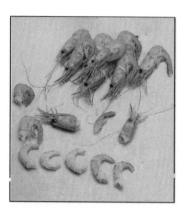

250 g (8 oz) unpeeled shrimps
60 g (2 oz/¼ cup) butter
1 small onion, finely chopped
155 ml (5 fl oz/⅔ cup) dry white wine
1 fish stock cube
1 bay leaf
few parsley stalks
3 strips lemon peel
3 teaspoons tomato purée (paste)
salt and pepper
30 g (1 oz/¼ cup) plain flour
grated nutmeg
155 ml (5 fl oz/⅔ cup) single (light) cream

Peel a few shrimps and reserve for garnish.

Process remainder in a blender or food processor until finely chopped. Melt half the butter in a saucepan, add onion and cook gently until soft. Stir in shrimps, cook for 4-5 minutes, then add wine and boil 2 minutes. Add 940 ml (1½ pints/3¾ cups) water, stock cube, bay leaf, parsley stalks, lemon peel, tomato purée (paste) and salt and pepper and bring to the boil. Simmer, uncovered, for 30 minutes, skimming surface. Strain through a nylon sieve. Discard bay leaf and parsley stalks, then put remaining solids in a blender or food processor with a little cooking liquid.

Work to make a purée. Press purée through a sieve into the cooking stock. Melt remaining butter in a clean pan, add flour and cook for 1 minute. Gradually stir in fish soup and season with nutmeg and salt and pepper. Bring to the boil, stirring constantly and simmer for 3 minutes, then stir in half the cream. Serve with remaining cream swirled on top and garnished with reserved shrimps scattered over.

Serves 4.

CRAB & SWEETCORN SOUP

940 ml (1½ pints/3¾ cups) chicken stock
1 small knob fresh root ginger, peeled
2 teaspoons light soy sauce
3 teaspoons dry sherry
470 g (15 oz) can creamed sweetcorn
salt and pepper
2 teaspoons cornflour
125 g (4 oz) crabmeat, well drained if canned
2 eggs, beaten
2 spring onions, finely chopped, to garnish

Put stock into a saucepan with ginger, cover and simmer for 15 minutes. Remove ginger, then stir in soy sauce, sherry, sweetcorn and salt and pepper and simmer for 5 minutes.

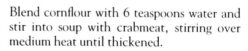

Blend cornflour with 6 teaspoons water and stir into soup with crabmeat, stirring over medium heat until thickened.

With soup at a gentle simmer, slowly pour in beaten eggs in a thin stream, stirring constantly: do not boil. Serve garnished with chopped spring onions.

Serves 4-6.

— POTAGE CRÈME DE FROMAGE —

30 g (1 oz/6 teaspoons) butter
1 onion, finely chopped
1 stick celery, finely chopped
30 g (1 oz/¼ cup) plain flour
500 ml (16 fl oz/2 cups) hot chicken stock
155 ml (5 fl oz/⅔ cup) milk
125 g (4 oz) camembert, rind removed
125 g (4 oz/½ cup) fromage frais
salt and pepper

PARSLEY CROÛTONS: 1 thick slice white bread, crusts
   removed
butter
2 tablespoons finely chopped fresh parsley

Melt butter in a saucepan, add onion and celery and cook gently for 5 minutes, until soft. Stir in flour and cook for 1 minute. Gradually stir in stock and milk, then return to a low heat and simmer for 15 minutes. Meanwhile, make croûtons. Toast bread on both sides until golden. Set aside to cool, then butter. Cut into small squares and then toss in parsley.

Cut the camembert into small pieces and add to soup with fromage frais. Stir for 2-3 minutes, until camembert melts. Add salt and pepper. Serve garnished with parsley croûtons.

Serves 4.

— COUNTRY MUSHROOM SOUP —

1 onion, thinly sliced
60 g (2 oz/⅓ cup) brown rice
1.5 litres (2½ pints/6 cups) chicken stock
45 g (1½ oz/9 teaspoons) butter
500 g (1 lb) mushrooms, wiped, trimmed and sliced
75 ml (2½ fl oz/⅓ cup) dry sherry
salt and pepper
parsley sprigs, to garnish

Put onion, rice and stock in a large saucepan and bring to the boil, then simmer for 25 minutes, until rice is tender.

Meanwhile, melt butter in another pan, add mushrooms and cook gently for about 10 minutes, until golden brown and most of the moisture has evaporated.

Transfer the mushrooms to stock, stir in sherry and season with salt and pepper. Simmer for 10 minutes, then serve garnished with sprigs of parsley.

Serves 6.

Variation: Use 2 varieties of mushrooms if available, such as button and open or chestnut mushrooms which have very good flavours. If wild mushrooms are available they can also be used.

PLOUGHMAN'S SOUP

45 g (1½ oz/9 teaspoons) butter
2 onions, chopped
30 g (1 oz/¼ cup) plain wholemeal flour
500 ml (16 fl oz/2 cups) chicken stock
250 ml (8 fl oz/1 cup) light ale
dash Worcestershire sauce
185 g (6 oz) Cheshire cheese, crumbled
salt and pepper
mild raw onion rings, to garnish

Melt butter in a saucepan, add onions and cook gently until soft. Stir in flour and cook for 1 minute. Remove from heat.

Gradually stir in stock and ale, then return to heat. Bring to the boil and simmer 5 minutes, until thickened. Flavour with Worcestershire sauce.

Stir in cheese a little at a time over a low heat, until melted, then add salt and pepper. Serve garnished with onion rings.

Serves 4.

ITALIAN BEAN & PASTA SOUP

6 teaspoons olive oil
1 onion, finely chopped
1 clove garlic, crushed
2 sticks celery, finely sliced
1 carrot, finely diced
3 teaspoons tomato purée (paste)
1.2 litres (2 pints/5 cups) beef stock
470 g (15 oz) can borlotti beans, drained and rinsed
90 g (3 oz) small pasta shapes
125 g (4 oz) shelled peas
salt and pepper

Heat oil in a large saucepan, add onion, garlic, celery and carrot.

Cook gently 5 minutes, until soft. Add tomato purée (paste), stock and beans and bring to the boil, then simmer 10 minutes.

Add pasta and peas and cook a further 7 minutes, until the pasta is just cooked. Add salt and pepper and serve hot.

Serves 4-6.

FRENCH ONION SOUP

30 g (1 oz/6 teaspoons) butter
6 teaspoons olive oil
500 g (1 lb) onions, thinly sliced
pinch caster sugar
1.2 litres (2 pints/5 cups) beef stock
1 bay leaf
salt and pepper

TO GARNISH: 4 thick slices French stick
1 teaspoon Dijon mustard
90 g (3 oz/¾ cup) Gruyère cheese, grated

Heat butter and oil together in a large saucepan. Add onions and sugar.

Cook over medium heat for about 20 minutes, stirring occasionally, until onions are deep golden brown. Add stock and bay leaf and slowly bring to the boil, then cover and simmer for 25 minutes. Remove bay leaf and add salt and pepper.

To make garnish, toast bread on each side, then spread with a little mustard. Ladle soup into 4 flameproof bowls and float a slice of bread in each. Pile cheese on to each slice and place bowls under a hot grill until cheese has melted and is bubbling. Serve at once.

Serves 4.

TOMATO & ORANGE SOUP

1 orange
3 teaspoons sunflower oil
1 small onion, chopped
1 clove garlic, crushed
750 g (1½ lb) ripe tomatoes, coarsely chopped
500 ml (16 fl oz/2 cups) chicken stock
1 teaspoon sugar
1 teaspoon chopped fresh basil
salt and pepper
60 ml (2 fl oz/¼ cup) double (thick) cream, whipped

Using a potato peeler, cut 4 strips of peel from orange and reserve for garnish. Grate remaining peel and squeeze the juice.

Heat oil in a saucepan, add onion and garlic and cook over low heat for 5 minutes until soft. Add tomatoes and grated peel and cook over medium heat for 5 minutes, until tomatoes become soft. Pour in stock and add sugar and basil, cover and simmer for 15 minutes.

Meanwhile, cut reserved orange peel into thin strips and drop into a pan of simmering water for 3 minutes, then drain and spread on a piece of absorbent kitchen paper. Purée soup in a blender or food processor, then press through a sieve. Return to pan and add salt and pepper. Stir in orange juice and reheat gently. Serve with a spoonful of whipped cream in each bowl, topped with a few shreds of orange peel.

Serves 4.

RICH COUNTRY CHICKEN SOUP

45 g (1½ oz/9 teaspoons) butter
125 g (4 oz) button mushrooms, chopped
45 g (1½ oz/⅓ cup) plain flour
625 ml (20 fl oz/2½ cups) strong chicken stock
625 ml (20 fl oz/2½ cups) milk
375 g (12 oz) cooked skinless chicken, diced
2 egg yolks
155 ml (5 fl oz/⅔ cup) single (thin) cream
salt and pepper

WATERCRESS DUMPLINGS: 125 g (4 oz/1 cup) self-raising
   flour
pinch dried mixed herbs
60 g (2 oz) shredded suet
1 bunch watercress, trimmed and finely chopped
1 small egg, beaten

Melt butter in a saucepan, add mushrooms and cook gently for 4-5 minutes. Stir in flour, and cook for 1 minute, then gradually add stock and milk. Bring to the boil, stirring constantly, then cover and simmer for 15 minutes. Meanwhile, make dumplings. Sift flour into a bowl, then mix in ½ teaspoon salt, herbs, suet and watercress. Add egg and 3 teaspoons water and mix to a soft dough. Divide into 24 pieces and roll into balls. Bring a pan of water to the boil, drop dumplings into the simmering liquid, cover and simmer for 10 minutes.

Take soup off heat and stir in chicken. Beat egg yolks and cream together, ladle in a little soup and mix quickly, then pour back into pan and heat gently until thickens: do not boil. Add salt and pepper if necessary. Lift dumplings out of water with a slotted spoon and add to the soup just before serving.

Serves 6.

Note: For extra flavour, cook the dumplings in stock instead of water.

CHICKEN NOODLE SOUP

60 g (2 oz) fine-cut vermicelli
1 tablespoon finely chopped fresh parsley

CHICKEN STOCK: 1 chicken carcass, raw or cooked, to
   include giblets but not liver
1 small onion, sliced
1 large carrot, sliced
1 stick celery, chopped
2-3 fresh parsley stalks
1 teaspoon salt
6 black peppercorns

To make stock, put chicken carcass into a large pan, cover with water and bring to the boil.

Skim off any scum that rises to surface. Add remaining stock ingredients and simmer gently 2½-3 hours, skimming as necessary. Strain and cool, then refrigerate overnight. Next day, remove any fat from surface. Measure 940 ml (1½ pints/3¾ cups) stock into a pan and reheat, seasoning if necessary.

Bring a pan of salted water to the boil, crumble in vermicelli and simmer for 4-5 minutes. Drain and rinse, then place in a soup tureen and pour over soup. Sprinkle with parsley before serving.

Serves 4.

ORIENTAL CHICKEN SOUP

1 clove garlic, finely chopped
1 piece lemon grass, halved lengthwise
1 carrot, cut into flowers
2 spring onions, chopped
60 g (2 oz) cooked chicken breast (fillet), shredded
60 g (2 oz) mange tout (snow peas), cut into strips

CHICKEN CONSOMMÉ: 125 g (4 oz) minced veal
1 carrot, finely chopped
1 stick celery, finely chopped
1 leek, trimmed, and finely sliced
1 thyme sprig and 1 bay leaf
1.8 litres (3 pints/7½ cups) chicken stock
salt and pepper
2 egg whites

To make consommé, put veal, vegetables, herbs and stock into a large saucepan with salt and pepper and begin to heat. Whisk egg whites and pour into pan, whisking constantly until a thick froth starts to form. When boiling, stop whisking and lower heat to maintain a very slow simmer: do not boil. Simmer, covered, for 1 hour. Line a large sieve or colander with muslin and stand it over a bowl. Draw scum back from surface of consommé.

Ladle clarified stock into the muslin-lined sieve. Place a piece of absorbent kitchen paper over surface to absorb any fat. Measure 940 ml (1½ pints/3¾ cups) consommé into a pan, add garlic and lemon grass and simmer for 15 minutes. Meanwhile, blanch carrot flowers for 2 minutes. Remove lemon grass and add spring onions, chicken and mange tout (snow peas) and simmer for 2 minutes. Add carrot flowers just before serving.

Serves 4.

MULLIGATAWNY

500 g (1 lb) piece shin of beef
5 cm (2 in) piece fresh root ginger, peeled
2 bay leaves
1 onion, chopped
1 teaspoon turmeric
½ teaspoon chilli powder
2 teaspoons coriander seeds, crushed
2 teaspoons cumin seeds, crushed
8 black peppercorns, crushed
1 small cooking apple, peeled, cored and chopped
1 carrot, sliced
30 g (1 oz/2 tablespoons) red lentils, rinsed
2 cloves garlic, chopped
salt
3 teaspoons lemon juice

Put beef into a large saucepan, pour in 1.9 litres (3 pints/7½ cups) water and bring to the boil. Skim surface, then add all remaining ingredients except lemon juice. Cover and simmer very gently for 2½-3 hours, until the beef is tender. Remove beef from the pan and set aside. Sieve soup into a bowl, rubbing vegetables through; discard pulp. Cool, then chill both the meat and stock.

To serve, remove solidified fat from surface of soup, then put into a pan and reheat. Cut beef into small pieces, add to soup with lemon juice and salt if necessary. Simmer for 5 minutes.

Serves 6.

BEEF & PASTA SOUP

185 g (6 oz) capellini (very fine spaghetti)

BEEF STOCK: 500 g (1 lb) shin of beef, cut into pieces
500 g (1 lb) marrow bones or knuckle of veal
1 onion, sliced
1 large carrot, sliced
bouquet garni
1 teaspoon salt
5 black peppercorns
1 bay leaf

PARMESAN BALLS: 30 g (1 oz/¼ cup) freshly grated
    Parmesan cheese
2 egg yolks

Preheat oven to 220C (425F/Gas 7). Put meat and bones in a roasting tin and roast for 15 minutes to brown, then turn meat and bones over and cook for a further 10 minutes. Transfer to a saucepan, add 1.8 litres (3 pints/7½ cups) water and bring to boil, skimming the surface. When only white foam is left, add onion, carrot, bouquet garni, salt, peppercorns and bay leaf. Cover and simmer very gently for 3 hours. (This should yield 1.2 litres (2 pints/5 cups) stock.)

Strain stock, cool and refrigerate. Next day, remove fat from surface and return stock to a pan. Reheat, seasoning if necessary. When simmering point is reached, break up pasta, drop into soup and cook for about 6 minutes, until just tender. To make Parmesan balls, mix cheese and egg yolks together, then drop ½ teaspoons of mixture over surface of soup. Cover and cook for about 4 minutes, until pasta is cooked. Serve at once.

Serves 6.

GOULASH SOUP

6 teaspoons vegetable oil
500 g (1 lb) lean stewing meat, cut into 0.5 cm (¼ in)
    cubes
1 large onion, thinly sliced
1 clove garlic, crushed
½ teaspoon ground cumin
2 teaspoons paprika
3 teaspoons plain flour
1.2 litres (2 pints/5 cups) beef stock
1 large potato
440 g (14 oz) can chopped tomatoes
salt and pepper
thick sour cream and paprika, to garnish

Heat oil in a large saucepan; add beef cubes and onion.

Cook over medium heat for 4-6 minutes until meat is browned and onion soft. Stir in garlic, cumin, paprika and flour and cook for 1 minute. Gradually add stock and bring to the boil, then cover and simmer for 2 hours.

Dice potato and add to soup with tomatoes and their juice and salt and pepper. Continue cooking for 30 minutes, until potatoes are tender. Serve garnished with spoonfuls of sour cream, sprinkled with paprika.

Serves 6.

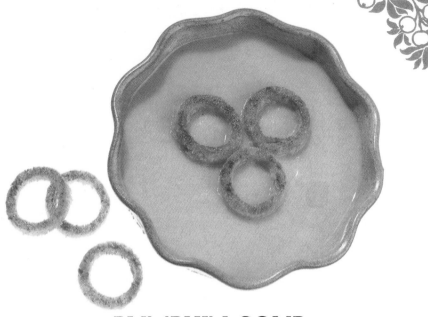

MANGE TOUT SOUP

30 g (1 oz/6 teaspoons) butter
5 spring onions, chopped
375 g (12 oz) mange tout (snow peas), trimmed
625 ml (20 fl oz/2½ cups) chicken stock
½ small lettuce, shredded
1 teaspoon sugar
1 tablespoon chopped fresh mint
155 ml (5 fl oz/⅔ cup) crème fraîche
salt and pepper

CROÛTONS: 2 slices bread
vegetable oil for frying

Melt butter in a saucepan, add spring onions and cook gently for 3-4 minutes.

Reserve 6 mange tout (snow peas), then chop remainder and add to pan with stock, lettuce and sugar and simmer for 5 minutes. Purée in a blender or food processor, then sieve and return to pan. Add mint, stir in crème fraîche and salt and pepper and reheat gently: do not boil. Do not reheat too long or the soup will loose its fresh colour.

Shred the reserved mange tout (snow peas) and blanch for 30 seconds, then drain. Cut bread into fancy shapes and fry in oil until crisp and golden. Drain on absorbent kitchen paper. Garnish the soup with the shreds of mange tout (snow peas) and croûtons.

Serves 4.

PUMPKIN SOUP

1.5 kg (3 lb) pumpkin
30 g (1 oz/6 teaspoons) butter
1 onion, chopped
625 ml (20 fl oz/2½ cups) chicken stock
1 teaspoon light brown sugar
good pinch grated nutmeg
¼ teaspoon paprika
salt and pepper
155 ml (5 fl oz/⅔ cup) single (light) cream

PAPRIKA NIBLETS: 3 slices bread
vegetable oil for frying
paprika

Discard pumpkin seeds and stringy bits.

Cut out pumpkin flesh and dice. Melt butter in a large saucepan, add onion and cook until soft. Add pumpkin, stock and sugar and bring to the boil, then cover and simmer for 30 minutes. Purée in a blender or food processor, then return to pan. Stir in nutmeg, paprika, salt and pepper and cream. Reheat gently while making the garnish.

Stamp out either attractive shapes from bread or make rings using 2 cutters, 1 slightly larger than the other. Heat enough oil to come to a depth of 0.5 cm (¼ in) in a frying pan and cook bread until golden. Drain on absorbent kitchen paper, then dust with paprika. Serve as a garnish to the soup.

Serves 6.

LOBSTER BISQUE

750 g (1½ lb) female lobster
90 g (3 oz/⅓ cup) butter
1 small onion, finely chopped
1 carrot, finely chopped
2 sticks celery, finely chopped
6 teaspoons brandy
155 ml (5 fl oz/⅔ cup) dry white wine
1.5 litres (2½ pints/6 cups) fish stock
3 strips lemon peel
45 g (1½ oz/3 tablespoons) long-grain rice
salt and pepper
2 slices toast, to garnish

Remove eggs from lobster tail and reserve.

Remove claws, and halve tail. Remove meat from body, discarding intestinal tube. Crack claws and remove meat. Discard stomach sac and gills from head part. Scoop out green 'cream' and reserve. Crush claw shells. Put softer body shell and feelers in a food processor and break up. Melt three-quarters of butter, add vegetables and cook 10 minutes. Stir in shells, pour over the brandy and ignite. When flames have subsided, add wine, three-quarters of stock and peel. Boil, then cover and simmer 25 minutes. Meanwhile, cook rice in remaining stock.

Reserve a little lobster meat, then put remainder in a food processor with the 'cream' and rice. Strain soup into a pan, add a little to the mixture in the processor and blend again. Whisk this fish mixture into the soup, season and gently reheat. Cut out 6 small rounds from the toast. Heat remaining butter in a small pan, add reserved fish eggs and cook to warm them through. Spoon on to toast for garnish and any remaining can be stirred into soup with reserved lobster.

Serves 6.

BOUILLABAISSE

1 kg (2 lb) mixed fish
500 g (1 lb) mixed shellfish
1 onion, sliced
1 carrot, sliced
1 stick celery, chopped
1 bay leaf
salt and pepper
6 teaspoons olive oil
2 cloves garlic, finely chopped
2 small leeks, trimmed and finely chopped
4 tomatoes, skinned and chopped
3 strips orange peel
good pinch saffron threads
1 sprig fresh thyme
slices of French bread, toasted

Clean and prepare the fish, removing the skin and bones and cutting into chunks. Shellfish can be left in their shells, but heads can be removed if desired. Put fish trimmings and bones in a large saucepan with the onion, carrot, celery and bay leaf. Pour in 1.5 litres (2½ pints/6 cups) water and bring to the boil. Add salt and pepper, remove any scum which rises to surface, cover and simmer for 30 minutes. Strain, discarding bones and vegetables.

Heat oil in pan, add garlic and leeks and cook over low heat for 5 minutes. Add tomatoes and cook for 5 minutes, then pour in stock and bring to the boil. Stir in orange peel, saffron and thyme. When soup is boiling, reduce heat and add white fish and simmer for 8 minutes. Add shellfish and cook for 5 minutes. Season if necessary. Serve accompanied with French toast.

Serves 6.

SMOKED SALMON & DILL SOUP

30 g (1 oz/6 teaspoons) butter
2 shallots, finely chopped
15 g (½ oz/6 teaspoons) plain flour
625 ml (20 fl oz/2½ cups) milk
½ fish stock cube
1 cucumber, peeled and chopped
185 g (6 oz) smoked salmon bits
1 tablespoon chopped fresh dill
155 ml (5 fl oz/⅔ cup) single (light) cream
salt and pepper

Melt butter in a pan, add shallots and cook until soft. Stir in flour and cook for 1 minute, then gradually stir in milk. Bring to boil and crumble in stock cube, then add cucumber.

Simmer stock for 10 minutes. Reserve a few of better bits of salmon for garnish, then chop remainder and add to soup and cook for 2-3 minutes.

Purée in a blender or food processor until smooth. Return to pan, add dill and cream and salt and pepper if necessary and gently reheat. Serve garnished with small pieces of reserved smoked salmon.

Serves 4.

CREAM OF ASPARAGUS SOUP

750 g (1½ lb) thin asparagus spears
45 g (1½ oz/9 teaspoons) butter
1 bunch spring onions, chopped
15 g (½ oz/6 teaspoons) plain flour
940 ml (1½ pints/3¾ cups) light chicken stock
2 egg yolks
155 ml (5 fl oz/⅔ cup) single (light) cream
salt and pepper
single (light) cream, to garnish

Wash asparagus, cut off tips and gently simmer in salted water for 3-5 minutes, until just tender. Drain and set aside. Cut off woody ends, scrape stalks to remove scales and then chop.

Melt butter in a saucepan, add chopped asparagus and spring onions and cook together for 5 minutes. Stir in flour and cook for 1 minute, then gradually add stock. Simmer for 20-25 minutes, until asparagus is tender.

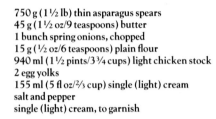

Cool soup slightly, then purée in a blender or food processor and sieve back into pan. Beat egg yolks in a bowl, then whisk in a little soup, and return to pan. Add cream and reheat gently until soup has a creamy texture, stirring. Add salt and pepper. Stir in reserved asparagus tips and heat for 2 minutes. Serve each portion with a swirl of cream.

Serves 6.

SEAFOOD PÂTÉ

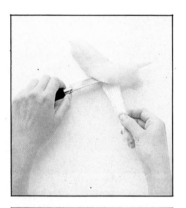

500 g (1 lb) white fish fillets
500 g (1 lb) raw prawns
90 g (3 oz) butter
6 spring onions, chopped
250 g (8 oz) scallops (optional)
1 clove garlic, crushed
2 tablespoons Cognac or brandy
125 ml (4 fl oz/½ cup) single cream
1 tablespoon lemon juice
1 teaspoon paprika
good pinch of cayenne pepper
lemon slices, fresh dill sprigs and peeled cooked
prawns, to serve

To remove the skin from the fish, place the
fish, skin side down and use a sharp knife to
separate flesh, pulling skin from side to side.
Cut the fish into chunks. Peel and de-vein
the prawns.

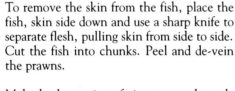

Melt the butter in a frying pan and gently
sauté the spring onions for 2 minutes. Add
the fish, prawns, scallops (if used) and
garlic. Cook, turning until the prawns turn
pink and the fish flakes.

Warm the Cognac, ignite and pour over the
fish mixture. When the flames subside, add
the cream. Stir in the lemon juice, paprika
and cayenne. Cool. Put the mixture into a
food processor and blend. Turn the mixture
into one large or several small serving
dishes, cover and chill until firm. Garnish
with lemon slices, sprigs of dill and prawns.
Serve with crackers, Melba toast or celery.

Serves 10.

HERB & GARLIC MUSSELS

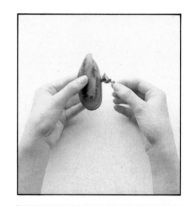

1 kg (2 lb) unshelled mussels
500 ml (16 fl oz/2 cups) water
125 g (4 oz) butter
2 cloves garlic, crushed
2 tablespoons chopped fresh parsley
1 tablespoon snipped fresh chives
1 tablespoon chopped fresh dill

Scrub the mussels well, removing the
beards. Cover with cold water and soak for
several hours. Discard any mussels with
broken shells. Drain.

Bring the water to the boil in a frying pan.
Add a layer of mussels and remove them
once they open. Add more mussels as the
cooked ones are removed. Discard any that
do not open. Lift off the top shell of each
mussel and discard. Beat the butter with the
remaining ingredients.

Spread the herb butter over each of the
mussels. Chill until ready to cook. Place
under a hot grill until tops colour. Serve hot.

*Makes about 30, depending on the size of the
mussels.*

SPANISH PRAWNS

500 g (1 lb) raw Mediterranean (king) prawns
6 tablespoons good olive oil or a mixture of olive and vegetable oil
1-2 small chillies, finely shredded
3 gloves garlic, crushed
salt
lemon wedges, to serve

Peel the prawns, leaving the tail intact. Cut along the back of each prawn, halfway through so it curls. Remove the vein.

Put the oil in a frying pan and add the chillies. Heat the oil until very hot, then add the prawns, garlic and salt, stirring until prawns are bright pink. Serve immediately with crusty bread and wedges of lemon. A bowl of Tartare Sauce may be placed alongside the prawns.

Serves 4.

TARTARE SAUCE: 6 tablespoons mayonnaise (use a good homemade mayonnaise)
3 spring onions, chopped
1 tablespoon drained capers
1 tablespoon finely chopped gherkins
1 tablespoon chopped fresh parsley

Combine all ingredients. Cover and chill until ready to serve with seafood.

GRILLED PRAWNS

8 raw Mediterranean (king) prawns, peeled
1 teaspoon olive or vegetable oil
2 tablespoons soy sauce
2 tablespoons ginger wine or dry sherry
squeeze of lemon juice
lemon slices, to serve

Remove the heads from the prawns. Cut each prawn along the back, taking care not to cut all the way through. Remove the vein.

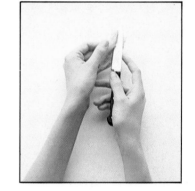

Open the prawns out flat and push a skewer through to hold each prawn open. Mix the oil, soy sauce, ginger wine and lemon juice together in a small bowl.

Brush the prawns with the soy sauce mixture. Grill on a barbecue or under a hot grill, basting constantly with the soy mixture until the prawns are cooked and well glazed. Alternatively, fry the prawns in an oiled frying pan, brushing with the soy mixture. Serve whole or cut into pieces with lemon slices.

Makes 8.

TARAMASALATA

2 thick slices of crusty bread, weighing about 180 g (6 oz)
125 g (4 oz) tarama (salted grey mullet roe)
1 clove garlic, crushed
1 tablespoon grated onion
1 egg yolk
2-3 tablespoons lemon juice
125 ml (4 fl oz/½ cup) olive oil
black olive and fresh chives, to garnish
crusty bread, to serve

Remove the crusts from the bread. Cover in cold water and soak for 10 minutes. Squeeze out the water.

Crumb the bread in a food processor. Remove. Place the tarama in the processor, add the garlic and onion and process until thoroughly mixed. Gradually add the breadcrumbs until the mixture is smooth. Blend in the egg yolk and 1 tablespoon of the lemon juice.

With the processor on, gradually pour in the olive oil, mixing until very creamy. Add more lemon juice to taste. Cover and chill. Garnish with a black olive and chives. Serve with crusty bread for dipping.

Serves 4 to 6.

Note: Tarama is the salted roe from grey mullet and is available from many delicatessens, and larger supermarkets.

SALMON MOUSSE

1 cucumber (use long one with few seeds)
440 g (14 oz) can red salmon, drained
1 tablespoon gelatine
125 ml (4 fl oz/½ cup) boiling water
½ teaspoon dry mustard
2 tablespoons white wine vinegar
1 teaspoon paprika
250 ml (8 fl oz/1 cup) single cream
lime slices, to serve

Trim the cucumber ends and cut lengthwise into thin slices using a mandolin or cutter. Line a long narrow 500 ml (16 fl oz/2 cup) loaf tin with the slices.

Mash salmon with a fork and remove any bones. Put the salmon flesh into a food processor and mix well. Dissolve the gelatine in the boiling water and pour over the salmon. Add the mustard, vinegar and paprika and blend well together until smooth.

Add the cream and blend until just mixed. Pour into the lined tin and chill until set. Turn out of the mould, cut into slices and serve on thin crispbreads or biscuits with lime slices.

Serves 4 to 6.

PARMA HAM ROULADES

60 g (2 oz) Ricotta cheese
60 g (2 oz) Stilton cheese
1 tablespoon thick sour cream
12 very thin slices Parma ham (prosciutto) or coppa or ham deluxe
1 pear, apple or fresh fig

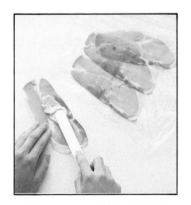

Blend both cheeses with the sour cream. Spread evenly on the thin slices of Parma ham (prosciutto), taking the mixture almost to the edges.

Peel the pear, cut into quarters and remove the core, then thinly slice. Place a piece of pear on each cheese-topped slice of prosciutto.

Roll up the ham. Place on a dish, cover and chill until ready to serve. Apples or fresh figs, when in season, may be used instead of the pear. Peel and slice the figs before using.

Makes 12.

CHICKEN SATAY

500 g (1 lb) skinned chicken breasts (fillets)
½ teaspoon sambal olek
1 teaspoon grated fresh root ginger
2 tablespoons lemon juice
3 tablespoons dark soy sauce
2 tablespoons honey
1 tablespoon peanut butter
125 ml (4 fl oz/½ cup) water
cherries and fresh parsley sprigs, to garnish

Cut the chicken into 2.5 cm (1 in) cubes and thread on to 15 bamboo skewers.

Put remaining ingredients, except the cherries and parsley, into a large frying pan or saucepan and heat, stirring well. Bring to the boil, then lower heat and add chicken skewers, cooking 1 layer at a time. Simmer for 10 minutes, basting occasionally, then remove chicken.

Repeat until all the skewers of chicken are cooked, basting from time to time. Simmer the sauce in the pan until it has reduced to about 180 ml (6 fl oz/¾ cup). Pour this over the chicken. Chill. The skewers may be garnished with cherries and fresh parsley sprigs. Serve cold.

Makes 15.

FISH PÂTÉ

850 ml (1½ pt/1 quart) water
60 ml (2 fl oz/¼ cup) dry vermouth
1 small carrot, chopped
1 small onion, chopped
1 stalk celery, chopped
1 teaspoon black peppercorns
1 teaspoon salt
Sprig of parsley
Small piece of fresh fennel and thyme
1 bay leaf
250 g (½ lb) fish fillets
2 teaspoons gelatine
2 tablespoons pimento, chopped
Salt and pepper
1 spring onion, finely chopped
Radishes, cucumber, lemon slices and red and black fish eggs

In a saucepan combine first 10 ingredients. Bring to boil; reduce heat and simmer 30 minutes. Add fish; poach 10 minutes until flesh flakes when tested with a fork.

Remove fillets; flake; cool. Reduce liquid to 375 ml (12 fl oz/1½ cups). Cool. When just warm, sprinkle gelatine on surface, stir to dissolve. In a food processor, purée fish, pimentos, spring onion, salt and pepper to texture that you prefer, gradually adding fish stock.

Pour into a 550 g (1¼ lb/3-cup) mould; refrigerate until set. Garnish with radishes, cucumber, lemon slices and red and black fish eggs. Store in the refrigerator up to 3 days.

Makes about 1 kg (2 lb).

POTTED SALMON

250 g (8 oz) smoked salmon
250 g (8 oz/1 cup) clarified butter
½ teaspoon ground white pepper
Pinch of salt
Sprigs of herbs, to decorate

In a food processor or blender, mix salmon, 185 g (6 oz/¾ cup) clarified butter and pepper.

Blend or process to a fine paste. Add salt to taste; refrigerate until firm. Press into a terrine or small attractive dishes.

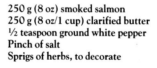

Decorate with sprigs of herbs. Melt remaining 60 g (2 oz/¼ cup) clarified butter, let cool slightly, spoon over potted salmon, making sure it covers completely. Store in refrigerator up to 1 week.

Makes about 450 g (1 lb).

GRAND MARNIER PÂTÉ

675 g (1½ lb) pork livers, cleaned, fibrous membrane removed
250 g (½ lb) bacon, cut into pieces
125 g (4 oz/½ cup) butter, cut into pieces
1 medium-size onion, finely chopped
60 ml (2 fl oz/¼ cup) Grand Marnier (or other orange liqueur)
2 teaspoons grated orange peel
2 tablespoons plain flour
2 eggs, beaten
2 teaspoons salt
1 teaspoon white pepper
½ teaspoon ground cloves
½ teaspoon ground allspice
½ teaspoon ground sage
¼ teaspoon each ground mace and ground nutmeg
3 tablespoons whipping cream
ORANGE GLAZE: 375 ml (12 fl oz/1½ cups) clear chicken soup
1½ teaspoons gelatine
2 tablespoons Grand Marnier (or other orange liqueur)
Thin slices of orange, small sprigs of rosemary, celery leaves, black olives and strips of red pepper, to decorate

Preheat oven to 180C (350F/Gas 5). In a food processor or blender, mix livers, bacon, butter and onion until a smooth purée, add liqueur and orange peel. It may be necessary to do this in batches.

In a bowl, mix together flour, eggs, salt, pepper, cloves, allspice, sage, mace, nutmeg, cream and puréed liver,

Pack into an ungreased 23 × 13-cm (9 × 5-in) loaf tin, terrine or pâté mould, Put tin into a larger, deep baking tin. Fill larger baking tin with hot water to level of pâté mixture. Bake for 2½ to 3 hours. Remove pâté from larger baking tin and cool in baking tin.

ORANGE GLAZE:
Warm chicken stock, sprinkle gelatine over surface and stir to dissolve slightly, add Grand Marnier. Decorate pâté with orange slices, small sprigs of rosemary, celery leaves, black olives and strips of red pepper.

Gently spoon the gelatine mixture over pâté a little at a time.

Store in the refrigerator – allow to set 24 hours before using. Will keep up to 3 weeks well-wrapped.

Makes about 1.5 kg (3 lb).

SALMON BAKED EGGS

4 slices smoked salmon
4 large eggs
salt and pepper
12 teaspoons crème fraîche
1-2 teaspoons chopped fresh dill
dill sprigs, to garnish
Melba toast, to serve

Preheat the oven to 180C (350F/ Gas 4). Trim a small strip 5 cm (2 in) long from each piece of salmon and reserve. Line 4 ramekins with the salmon slices and carefully crack an egg into each one. Season well with salt and pepper.

Mix together crème fraîche and chopped dill and divide equally between the ramekins. Place the ramekins in a roasting tin half filled with hot water and bake in the oven for 15 minutes.

Roll reserved salmon strips into small curls and garnish each ramekin with a salmon roll and a sprig of dill. Serve the ramekins with Melba toast.

Serves 4.

PARMA HAM WITH FIGS

125 g (4 oz) Parma ham, very thinly sliced
4 fresh figs
4 fig or vine leaves
1 teaspoon clear honey
4 teaspoons fresh lime juice
8 teaspoons olive oil
1 teaspoon pink peppercorns, crushed slightly
rind of 1 lime

Trim any excess fat from Parma ham and cut in half lengthways. Cut figs into quarters. Arrange fig leaves on individual plates and pleat the ham in a neat shape on top. Set figs in the ham nest.

Combine honey, lime juice, oil and peppercorns and whisk well. Spoon generously over figs and ham and garnish each portion with a few shreds of lime rind.

Serves 4.

TROUT QUENELLES

2 large trout, filleted and skinned

1 egg white

2 teaspoons chopped fresh dill

3 teaspoons thick sour cream

pinch ground nutmeg

salt and pepper

500 ml (16 fl oz/2 cups) fish stock

3 teaspoons lemon juice

½ cucumber, grated

1 egg yolk

125 ml (4 fl oz/½ cup) double (thick) cream

½ teaspoon cornflour

TO GARNISH:

cucumber

lemon slices

dill sprigs

Put trout, egg white, dill, sour cream, nutmeg and salt and pepper in a blender or food processor and process for 30 seconds.

Pour fish stock and lemon juice into a saucepan and bring to the boil. Reduce the heat until the stock is just simmering. Using 2 dessert spoons, shape trout mixture into 8 lozenges and put into the stock. Poach for 3-4 minutes until quenelles rise to top of pan. Remove and keep warm.

Boil the poaching liquid until only 155 ml (5 fl oz/⅔ cup) remains, add cucumber and boil for 5 minutes until tender. Pour into a blender or food processor and process until smooth.

Mix together egg yolk, cream and cornflour and pour a little of the cucumber sauce on top. Mix well, then return to the pan with the rest of the sauce. Heat gently, stirring until slightly thickened.

Pour the sauce over the bases of 4 plates and arrange the quenelles on top. Garnish and serve.

Serves 4.

GRILLED FLORIDA COCKTAIL

2 ruby grapefruit

1 grapefruit

3 oranges

1 lime

4 teaspoons sweet sherry

8 teaspoons soft brown sugar

4 teaspoons butter

parsley sprigs and lime slices, to garnish

Halve grapefruit, then remove the flesh using a grapefruit knife, and cut into segments. Reserve 4 of the grapefruit skins.

Cut away top and bottom from the oranges and lime and, working from the top, cut away all the skin and pith. Reserving any juices, cut the flesh into segments, discarding the tough membranes. Mix together the orange and lime with the grapefruit segments.

Arrange the fruit back in the grapefruit skins and spoon a teaspoon of sherry over each. Sprinkle with sugar and top with a teaspoon of butter. Put under a hot grill until the sugar has melted. Top with the reserved fruit juices and serve at once, garnished with sprigs of parsley and slices of lime.

Serves 4.

HERB BAKED EGGS

4 thin slices ham
3 large eggs
1 teaspoon prepared mustard
60 ml (2 fl oz/¼ cup) Greek yogurt
90 g (3 oz) mature Cheddar cheese, finely grated
2 teaspoons chopped fresh chives
2 teaspoons chopped fresh parsley
fresh herbs, to garnish
slices of hot buttered toast, to serve

Preheat the oven to 180C (350F/ Gas 4). Line 4 greased ramekins with ham slices. Beat together eggs, mustard and yogurt.

Stir 60 g (2 oz/¼ cup) of the cheese into the egg mixture. Mix together chives and parsley and add half to the mixture. Stir well, then spoon into prepared ramekins. Sprinkle with remaining cheese and herbs and bake in the oven for 25-30 minutes until golden and set.

Serve in the ramekins, garnished with fresh herbs. Serve the baked eggs with slices of hot buttered toast.

Serves 4.

SAUSAGE-STUFFED MUSHROOMS

375 g (12 oz) low-fat sausagemeat
220 g (7 oz) can chopped tomatoes, drained
2 teaspoons tomato purée (paste)
2 teaspoons sweet pickle, chopped
salt and pepper
6 large flat field mushrooms
1 tablespoon vegetable oil
125 g (4 oz) Mozzarella cheese, thinly sliced
basil sprigs, to garnish

Fry sausagemeat in a non-stick pan for 3 minutes, then stir in drained tomatoes, tomato purée (paste) and sweet pickle. Bring to the boil and cook until thickened. Season to taste with salt and pepper.

Brush tops of mushrooms with oil and place under a hot grill for 1 minute to warm through.

Turn mushrooms over and pile sausage mixture on top. Cover with slices of Mozzarella cheese and return to the grill until bubbly. Serve garnished with basil.

Serves 6.

STRUDEL TRIANGLES

155 g (5 oz) chicken, cooked
90 g (3 oz/¾ cup) feta cheese, crumbled
1 small avocado pear, chopped
2 teaspoons creamed horseradish sauce
salt and pepper
6 sheets filo pastry
60 g (2 oz/⅓ cup) butter, melted
basil sprigs, to garnish

Preheat the oven to 220C (425F/ Gas 7). Finely chop chicken, then mix with feta cheese, avocado pear and horseradish sauce. Season with salt and pepper.

Brush 3 of the sheets of filo pastry with melted butter and lay a second sheet on top of each. Cut each double sheet into six 7.5 cm (3 in) wide strips. Put a teaspoon of chicken filling onto the top corner of each strip and brush the pastry with butter. Fold the pastry and filling over at right angles to make a triangle and continue folding in this way along the strip of pastry to form a neat triangular pastry parcel.

Brush the parcels with butter and place on a baking sheet. Repeat with remaining strips. Bake the parcels in the oven for 10-15 minutes until golden brown. Serve warm, garnished with sprigs of fresh basil.

Makes 18.

PRAWN BARQUETTES

125 g (4 oz/1 cup) plain flour
pinch salt
3 teaspoons finely grated Parmesan cheese
90 g (3 oz/⅓ cup) butter
1 egg yolk
prawns and lemon triangles, to garnish
FILLING:
45 g (1½ oz/9 teaspoons) butter
185 g (6 oz) button mushrooms, sliced
155 ml (5 fl oz/⅔ cup) thick sour cream
1-2 teaspoons dry sherry
90 g (3 oz) prawns, chopped
2-3 teaspoons fresh chopped chives

Put flour, salt, cheese and butter into a blender or food processor and process for 30 seconds. Add egg yolk and 4 teaspoons water and process until mixture binds together. Wrap in plastic wrap and leave to rest in the refrigerator for 20 minutes. Meanwhile, preheat the oven to 220C (425F/Gas 7).

Roll out pastry on a lightly floured surface until very thin. Lift pastry, using a rolling pin, and lay it over 12 barquette tins. Press down lightly and roll over tins to trim. Press pastry down in tins. Prick base of each tin and stack them one on top of each other 3 tins high. Top each stack with an empty tin.

Bake in the oven for 15 minutes. Remove from oven and unstack tins. Return single layer of tins to oven for 2-3 minutes to crisp. Leave to cool.

To make filling, melt butter in a pan and fry mushrooms for 1 minute. Pour in cream and bring to boil, stirring continuously until thickened. Add sherry, prawns and chives and mix well. Allow to cool slightly, then spoon into barquettes. Garnish each portion with prawns and triangles of lemon.

Makes 12.

KEDGEREE

375 g (12 oz) smoked cod fillets, skinned
250 g (8 oz) kipper fillets, skinned
60 g (2 oz/¼ cup) wild rice
125 g (4 oz/¾ cup) brown rice
60 g (2 oz/¼ cup) butter
1 onion, chopped
2 teaspoons curry powder
2 hard-boiled eggs, diced
juice of ½ lemon
2 tablespoons chopped fresh parsley
155 ml (5 fl oz/⅔ cup) thick sour cream
salt and pepper
lemon wedges and parsley sprigs, to garnish

Poach fish in 625 ml (20 fl oz/2½ cups) water for 10-12 minutes until just cooked, then remove with a slotted spoon, reserving the cooking liquor. Flake the fish.

Put wild rice in a saucepan, cover with the fish cooking liquor, bring to the boil and simmer for 15 minutes. Add brown rice and a further 500 ml (16 fl oz/2 cups) water. Cover and simmer for 25 minutes, then drain.

Melt butter in a large frying pan and cook onion until slightly softened and transparent. Add curry powder and rice and cook for 2-3 minutes. Stir in flaked fish, eggs, lemon juice, parsley and cream and heat through. Season to taste with salt and pepper. Serve the kedgeree at once while piping hot, garnished with lemon wedges and sprigs of parsley.

Serves 4.

COULIBIAC

45 g (1½ oz/9 teaspoons) butter
1 onion, diced
125 g (4 oz) button mushrooms, sliced
90 g (3 oz/3 tablespoons) rice, cooked
2 tablespoons chopped fresh parsley
salt and pepper
375 g (12 oz) fresh salmon fillet
185 ml (6 fl oz/¾ cup) dry white wine
500 g (1 lb) packet puff pastry
1 egg, beaten
1 hard-boiled egg, chopped
315 ml (10 fl oz/1¼ cups) thick sour cream

Preheat the oven to 220C (425F/Gas 7). In a frying pan, melt butter and gently sauté onion until slightly softened. Add mushrooms and cook for 5 minutes. Stir in rice and parsley. Season and cool.

Place salmon in a shallow pan with wine and 125 ml (4 fl oz/½ cup) water and simmer for 10 minutes until just cooked. Remove salmon and flake.

Roll out 440 g (14 oz) of pastry into a 37.5 x 25 cm (15 x 10 in) rectangle and brush with beaten egg. Arrange half mushroom mixture down centre third of pastry, leaving a 5 cm (2 in) strip top and bottom. Top with half the salmon, then chopped egg. Cover with remaining salmon and mushroom mixture. Fold sides of pastry up and over filling so that edges overlap, and fold the ends over the top. Brush with beaten egg.

Turn over and place on a baking sheet with edges underneath. Roll out remaining pastry and cut out fish shapes. Brush the pastry with egg, make a small hole in the top and decorate with fish shapes. Bake for 25 minutes until golden. Serve with thick sour cream.

Serves 6-8.

SMOKED FISH LASAGNE

500 g (1 lb) smoked fish fillets, such as haddock

625 ml (20 fl oz/2½ cups) milk

4 carrots, cut into small dice

4 sticks celery, cut into small dice

90 g (3 oz/½ cup) butter

6 sheets lasagne verde

3 teaspoons chopped fresh parsley

salt and pepper

60 g (2 oz/½ cup) plain flour

freshly grated nutmeg

30 g (1 oz/6 teaspoons) grated Parmesan cheese

lime twist and sprig of parsley, to garnish

Put fish and milk into a large saucepan. Bring to the boil, then simmer gently until fish is cooked.

Put carrots and celery into a saucepan with 30 g (1 oz/6 teaspoons) butter and 500 ml (16 fl oz/2 cups) water. Bring to the boil, then simmer until vegetables are tender. Meanwhile, in a large pan of boiling salted water, cook lasagne until just tender. Drain and spread out on a tea towel. Drain fish, reserving cooking liquid, and flake into a bowl. Drain vegetables, reserving liquid, and add to fish with parsley. Season with salt and pepper.

Preheat oven to 190C (375F/Gas 5). Make a Béchamel sauce, see page 26, left, with remaining butter, flour, vegetable water and milk from fish. Season with salt, pepper and nutmeg. Arrange a layer of lasagne in the base of an ovenproof dish. Cover with one-third of fish mixture then one-third of sauce. Repeat layers twice, ending with sauce. Sprinkle with Parmesan cheese. Bake in the oven for 25 minutes. Serve, garnished with lime twist and parsley.

Serves 4-6.

FISH & PASTA PIE

375 g (12 oz) smoked haddock

375 g (12 oz) fresh haddock

440 ml (14 fl oz/1¾ cups) milk

185 g (6 oz/1¼ cups) macaroni

30 g (1 oz/6 teaspoons) butter

30 g (1 oz/¼ cup) plain flour

1 teaspoon lemon juice

3 hard-boiled eggs, sliced

3 teaspoons chopped fresh parsley

salt and pepper

250 ml (8 fl oz/1 cup) Greek strained yogurt

2 eggs, beaten

90 g (3 oz/¾ cup) grated Cheddar cheese

lemon slices and sprigs of parsley, to garnish

Put fresh and smoked haddock in a saucepan with milk and 315 ml (10 fl oz/1¼ cups) water. Poach fish for 5-10 minutes until flesh flakes when tested with a fork.

In a large saucepan of boiling salted water, cook macaroni until tender.

Preheat oven to 190C (375F/Gas 5). In a heavy saucepan, melt butter. Stir in flour and cook for 2 minutes, stirring over gentle heat. Remove from heat and stir in 315 ml (10 fl oz/1¼ cups) of cooking liquid. Return to heat and stir until thick and smooth. Add lemon juice, hard-boiled eggs, and parsley. Season with salt and pepper. Pour mixture into an ovenproof dish.

In a bowl, mix together yogurt and beaten eggs. Stir in macaroni and 60 g (2 oz/½ cup) cheese. Pour over fish mixture. Sprinkle with remaining cheese. Bake in the oven for 25-30 minutes until golden brown. Serve, garnished with lemon slices and sprigs of parsley.

Serves 4-6.

— BARBECUED TROUT IN LEAVES —

4 trout or 8 small red mullet, cleaned
8 vine leaves
1 teaspoon arrowroot
fennel sprigs and bay leaves, to garnish
MARINADE:
6 teaspoons olive oil
shredded peel from 1 Seville orange
6 teaspoons freshly squeezed orange juice
1 clove garlic, crushed
6 cardamom pod seeds, removed and crushed
½ teaspoon salt
½ teaspoon black pepper
1 teaspoon Dijon mustard
2 bay leaves
3 teaspoons chopped fresh fennel

Remove scales from the fish and cut off fins and gills using sharp scissors. Rinse under running water and dry on absorbent kitchen paper, then score the flesh on each side.

To make marinade, mix olive oil, orange peel, juice, garlic, cardamom seeds, salt, pepper, mustard, bay leaves and fennel together.

Immerse fish in marinade and turn to coat evenly. Cover with plastic wrap and leave in a cool place for 1 hour.

Preheat a hot grill. Take fish out of marinade and loosely wrap each in a vine leaf. Arrange fish on grill rack and cook for 6 minutes, turning once.

Unwrap each fish and arrange on a serving plate. Add juices from pan to remaining marinade and blend together with arrowroot. Put in a saucepan and bring to the boil, stirring, and cook for 1 minute, until thickened and glossy.

Pour sauce over fish and garnish with fennel and bay leaves.

Serves 4.

— BUTTERED HERB SOLE FILLETS —

8 Dover sole fillets, cut in half lengthwise
125 g (4 oz/½ cup) unsalted butter, softened
4 teaspoons chopped fresh tarragon
4 teaspoons plain flour
6 teaspoons single (light) cream
fennel sprigs, to garnish
MARINADE:
250 ml (8 fl oz/1 cup) dry white wine
3 teaspoons chopped fresh fennel
1 eating apple, peeled and grated
2 teaspoons caster sugar
½ teaspoon salt
½ teaspoon cayenne pepper

To make marinade, mix wine, fennel, apple, sugar, salt and cayenne together in a casserole or shallow flameproof dish, stirring until well blended.

Add sole fillets and turn in marinade to coat evenly. Cover with plastic wrap and leave the fish in a cool place for 2 hours.

In a bowl, blend together butter and tarragon. Lift sole fillets out of marinade and lay flat on a board. Spread half of each fillet with herbed butter, then roll up firmly and secure each with cocktail stick.

Arrange rolled fillets in dish with marinade, cover and cook over a gentle heat for 5-6 minutes, until fish is cooked through and flakes easily. Lift fillets out carefully, arrange on a warm serving dish and keep warm.

Blend flour and cream together in a bowl, then strain marinade into bowl, stirring well. Return to saucepan, bring to the boil and cook for 1 minute. Pour sauce around fish fillets and garnish with fennel sprigs.

Serves 4-5.

— FRENCH COUNTRY COD STEAKS —

4 middle-cut cod steaks, 2.5 cm (1 in) thick
30 g (1 oz/6 teaspoons) butter
15 g (½ oz/6 teaspoons) plain flour
tarragon sprigs, to garnish
MARINADE:
1 red pepper (capsicum)
1 yellow pepper (capsicum)
16 black olives, stoned
4 tomatoes, skinned, seeded and sliced
2 courgettes (zucchini), sliced
1 red onion, sliced
1 clove garlic, crushed
6 teaspoons olive oil
155 ml (5 fl oz/⅔ cup) strong cider
½ teaspoon salt
½ teaspoon black pepper
1 teaspoon French mustard
4 teaspoons chopped fresh tarragon

To make marinade, place peppers (capsicums) on a grill rack and cook for 10 minutes, turning occasionally, until skins have charred and flesh is tender. Cool, then peel off skins, and remove stalks and seeds. Cut peppers (capsicums) into strips and place in an ovenproof dish.

Add olives, tomatoes, courgettes (zucchini), onion, garlic, oil, cider, salt, pepper, mustard and tarragon, stirring until well mixed.

Immerse cod steaks in marinade and turn to coat evenly. Cover and leave in a cool place for 1 hour.

Preheat oven to 200C (400F/Gas 6). Cook cod steaks in marinade for 25-30 minutes, until cooked and flake easily. Lift out on to a plate and remove bones and skin.

Blend butter and flour together, stir into marinade, then bring to the boil and cook for 2 minutes.

Arrange cod steaks on a serving plate, pour over marinade and garnish with sprigs of tarragon.

Serves 4.

— MUSSELS WITH BASIL SAUCE —

32 fresh mussels
parsley sprigs or basil, to garnish
MARINADE:
9 teaspoons olive oil
3 teaspoons raspberry vinegar
3 teaspoons chopped fresh parsley
2 teaspoons pink peppercorns, crushed
½ teaspoon salt
½ teaspoon black pepper
1 teaspoon Dijon mustard
SAUCE:
60 g (2 oz/¼ cup) butter, softened
15 g (½ oz/6 teaspoons) plain flour
6 teaspoons chopped fresh basil
6 teaspoons single (light) cream

Scrub mussels thoroughly under running water and scrape shells clean with a small knife if necessary. Pull beards or thin strands off from side of shells. Discard any that are open.

Place mussels in a stainless steel saucepan. Cover and heat very gently until all shells have opened. Remove pan from heat; discard any shells that have not opened.

To make marinade, mix oil, vinegar, parsley, peppercorns, salt, pepper and mustard together, stirring until well blended. Pour marinade over mussels, stir well and leave for 1 hour.

Return mussels to heat, bring to the boil and cook for 1 minute. Take mussels, 1 at a time, remove empty side of shell and arrange remainder in a shallow serving dish.

To make sauce, blend together butter and flour, then add basil and whisk into marinade in saucepan. Add 90 ml (3 fl oz/⅓ cup) water and bring to the boil.

Stir in cream, then pour sauce over mussels in dish. Garnish with fresh parsley sprigs or basil leaves.

Serves 4-6.

SALMON IN FILO PASTRY

4 salmon steaks, about 500 g (1 lb), skinned and boned
90 g (3 oz/⅓ cup) unsalted butter
185 g (6 oz) oyster mushrooms, thinly sliced
4 sheets filo pastry, thawed if frozen
2 teaspoons arrowroot
3 teaspoons single (light) cream
fennel sprigs and pink peppercorns, to garnish
MARINADE:
2 teaspoons light soft brown sugar
6 teaspoons rosé wine
6 teaspoons raspberry vinegar
2 teaspoons pink peppercorns, crushed
4 teaspoons chopped fresh fennel
4 teaspoons chopped fresh oregano

Mix the marinade ingredients together, pour over the salmon in a shallow dish and turn to coat evenly. Cover with plastic wrap and leave in a cool place for 1 hour.

Preheat oven to 200C (400F/Gas 6). Melt 30 g (1 oz/6 teaspoons) butter in a small saucepan, add mushrooms, reserving a few for garnish, and fry quickly. Drain, reserving the liquid, then cool.

Melt remaining butter. Brush each sheet of filo pastry with melted butter and fold in half. Take 1 salmon steak at a time, drain well and place in centre of 1 folded piece of pastry. Top with one quarter mushroom slices and wrap up neatly. Place on a buttered baking sheet; repeat to make 4 parcels. Brush with remaining butter.

Cook for 15 minutes, until pastry is crisp and lightly browned. Mix marinade, mushroom liquid and arrowroot in a pan. Bring to boil and cook 1 minute; stir in cream.

Garnish salmon and serve with cream sauce.

Serves 4.

SEAFOOD KEBABS

375 g (12 oz) thick end monkfish, cut into bite-size pieces
3 plaice fillets, cut into thin strips
3 courgettes (zucchini), cut into bite-size pieces
1 small yellow pepper (capsicum), seeded and cut into bite-size pieces
12 large prawns, peeled
MARINADE:
¼ teaspoon powdered saffron
finely grated peel of 1 lime
3 teaspoons freshly squeezed lime juice
3 teaspoons clear honey
1 teaspoon green peppercorns, crushed
6 teaspoons white vermouth
90 ml (3 fl oz/⅓ cup) grapeseed oil
½ teaspoon salt
½ teaspoon black pepper
6 fresh bay leaves
3 teaspoons chopped fresh dill
GARNISH:
bay leaves
6 lime wedges
dill sprigs

To make marinade, mix all the ingredients together. Add monk-fish, plaice, courgettes (zucchini), pepper (capsicum) and prawns to marinade. Turn vegetables and fish carefully in marinade to coat evenly. Cover with plastic wrap and leave in a cool place for 1 hour. Meanwhile, soak 6 fine wooden skewers in cold water. Prepare barbecue or preheat grill.

Thread alternate pieces of each fish, with courgette (zucchini) and pepper (capsicum) in between, on to skewers with a bay leaf at the end of each. Cook for 5-8 minutes, turning only once and brushing with more marinade if necessary.

Arrange on a warmed serving dish and serve at once, garnished with fresh bay leaves, lime wedges and sprigs of dill.

Serves 6.

SPICY SCALLOPS

12 scallops, cleaned	
90 ml (3 fl oz/⅓ cup) cider	
15 g (½ oz/6 teaspoons) plain flour	
15 g (½ oz/3 teaspoons) butter	
2 teaspoons finely grated lemon peel	
6 teaspoons lemon juice	
3 teaspoons chopped fresh dill	
MARINADE:	
90 ml (3 fl oz/⅓ cup) sour cream	
½ teaspoon ground cumin	
½ teaspoon ground cinnamon	
½ teaspoon turmeric	
1 teaspoon grated fresh root ginger	
2 teaspoons clear honey	
½ teaspoon salt	
½ teaspoon black pepper	
GARNISH:	
toast triangles	
dill sprigs	
lemon wedges	

Place scallops and cider in a saucepan; poach gently for 1 minute.

To make marinade, mix sour cream, cumin, cinnamon, turmeric, ginger, honey, salt and pepper together, stirring until well blended.

Lift scallops out of liquor with a slotted spoon and slice thinly. Add to marinade and turn to coat evenly. Cover with plastic wrap and leave for 1 hour.

Whisk flour and butter into poaching liquor in saucepan, then bring to the boil, whisking, until sauce thickens. Stir in scallops, marinade, lemon peel and juice and dill and cook gently until mixture comes to boil, stirring occasionally.

Divide scallops between 6 shells or individual serving dishes and garnish with triangles of toast, dill sprigs and lemon wedges.

Serves 6.

TROUT IN ASPIC

4 trout, each about 250 g (8 oz), rinsed	
90 ml (3 fl oz / ⅓ cup) mayonnaise	
2 teaspoons tomato purée (paste)	
6 teaspoons lemon juice	
15 g (½ oz / 3 teaspoons) gelatine	
1 cucumber, very thinly sliced	
lemon wedges, to garnish	
MARINADE:	
1 red onion, sliced	
60 g (2 oz / ½ cup) bulb fennel, chopped	
2 bay leaves	
6 teaspoons chopped fresh parsley	
315 ml (10 fl oz / 1¼ cups) dry white wine	
½ teaspoon each salt and black pepper	

Mix the marinade, then pour over trout in a shallow ovenproof dish. Cover and leave in a cool place for 2-3 hours. Mix mayonnaise and tomato purée (paste) together.

Preheat oven to 190C (375F/Gas 5). Cook trout for 15-20 minutes, until flesh flakes easily. Cool. Lift 1 trout out of marinade, peel off skin and remove fins, leaving head and tail intact. Remove top fillet; place lower fillet on a plate. Cut through centre bone of lower fillet at head and tail end, then lift off bones. Spread fillet with one quarter mayonnaise; replace top fillet. Repeat with remaining trout.

Strain marinade into a jug and make up to 440 ml (14 fl oz/1¾ cups) with water. Add lemon juice and blend 9 teaspoons of marinade with gelatine in a small bowl. Melt over pan of hot water, stir into remaining marinade; leave until beginning to thicken.

Sprinkle cucumber with salt, leave 15 minutes, rinse and pat dry. Brush trout with marinade and arrange overlapping cucumber slices to cover. Glaze with marinade; leave to set. Garnish.

Serves 4.

COCONUT SPICED COD

four 185-250 g (6-8 oz) cod steaks
salt and pepper
2 tablespoons vegetable oil
1 onion, chopped
125 g (4 oz/1⅓ cups) desiccated coconut
5 cm (2 in) piece fresh root ginger, grated
2 cloves garlic, crushed
2 green chillies, seeded and chopped
½ teaspoon chilli powder
grated peel and juice of 1 lemon
2 tablespoons chopped fresh coriander
2 tomatoes, skinned, seeded and diced
oregano leaves, to garnish

Wash cod steaks and pat dry with absorbent kitchen paper. Place in a greased ovenproof dish and sprinkle with salt and pepper. Heat oil in a frying pan, add onion and fry, stirring, for about 5 minutes or until soft. Stir in coconut, ginger, garlic, chillies and chilli powder and fry, stirring, for 3-5 minutes, until golden brown.

Stir in lemon peel and juice and simmer, covered, for 10 minutes to soften coconut. Preheat oven to 160C (325F/Gas 3). Stir coriander and tomatoes into coconut mixture and spoon over cod steaks. Cook for 20-25 minutes, until fish flakes easily. Serve hot, garnished with oregano leaves.

Serves 4.

Note: Cover with foil during cooking if coconut begins to brown too much.

MADRAS CURRIED CRABS

4 medium cooked crabs
3 tablespoons vegetable oil
1 onion, finely chopped
3 cloves garlic, finely sliced
2.5 cm (1 in) piece fresh root ginger, grated
1 beef tomato, skinned and chopped
3 fresh green chillies, seeded and chopped
2 tablespoons desiccated coconut, toasted
2 tablespoons Almond Masala
250 ml (8 fl oz/1 cup) Coconut Milk

Remove large claws from crabs and crack to make eating easier. Twist off small claws.

Pull out body sections from shells, remove finger-shaped gills and discard. Cut body sections in half with a large sharp knife or cleaver and use a skewer to remove all the white meat. Remove the greyish white stomach sac behind each head and any green coloured matter and discard. Scrape out creamy brown meat from shells and add to white meat. Use a heavy weight to tap round underside of shells and break round natural dark line, discarding the broken bits of shell. Wash main shells and set aside.

Heat oil in a large frying pan, add onion and fry, stirring frequently, for about 8 minutes or until soft and golden. Add garlic and ginger and fry for 1 minute. Stir in tomato, chillies, coconut, almond masala, coconut milk and reserved crab meat. Add crab claws and simmer, covered, for 6-8 minutes, until heated through. Spoon the mixture into crab shells and serve hot.

Serves 4.

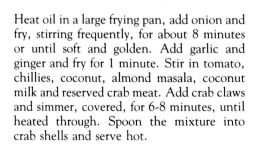

ROAST STUFFED TURKEY

4 kg (8 lb) oven-ready turkey with giblets
250 g (8 oz/4¼ cups) soft white breadcrumbs
1 large onion, finely chopped
3 sticks celery, finely chopped
finely grated peel and juice of 1 lemon
8 plums, chopped
155 ml (5 fl oz/⅔ cup) red wine
500 g (1 lb/2 cups) chestnut purée
3 teaspoons each of chopped fresh sage, thyme and
    oregano
salt and pepper
500 g (1 lb) rashers fat streaky bacon
60 g (2 oz/½ cup) plain flour

Cover the whole turkey with rashers of streaky bacon to help keep it moist during cooking.

Remove giblets from turkey, place in a saucepan with 625 ml (20 fl oz/2½ cups) water and bring to boil. Cover and simmer for 1 hour. Strain stock into a bowl; reserve liver. In a saucepan, place breadcrumbs, onion, celery, lemon peel and juice, plums and wine. Bring to boil, stirring, and cook for 1 minute. Put chestnut purée, herbs, salt and pepper to taste and turkey liver into a food processor fitted with a metal blade. Process until smooth. Add breadcrumb mixture and process until evenly blended.

Preheat oven to 190C (375F/Gas 5). Cook turkey in the oven for 2 hours, remove from oven; remove bacon if you require it for serving, and cover turkey and tin with thick foil. Return to oven for a further 1-1½ hours until turkey is tender and only clear juices run when pierced with a sharp pointed knife between legs of turkey. Leave to stand in tin for 20 minutes before removing. Remove any skewers or trussing string and place turkey on a warmed serving dish. Chop crispy bacon finely and serve with turkey.

Place ⅓ stuffing into neck end of turkey, pull over flap of skin and secure under turkey with skewers or string. Fill cavity of turkey with remaining stuffing, pull skin over parson's nose and secure with skewers or string. Truss turkey with string, securing wings and legs closely to body, and place in a roasting tin.

To make gravy, blend flour and a little stock together in a pan until smooth. Pour remaining stock into roasting tin, stir well, strain gravy into saucepan with flour mixture. Bring to boil, stirring until thickened; cook for 2 minutes. Season to taste with salt and pepper and pour into a gravy boat. Serve turkey with bread sauce, chipolata sausages, crisp bacon and gravy.

Serves 10.

GOOSEBERRY GOOSE

4 kg (8 lb) oven-ready goose, with giblets
12 rashers streaky bacon
3 teaspoons Dijon mustard
250 ml (8 fl oz/1 cup) elderflower wine
500 g (1 lb) gooseberries, cooked
3 teaspoons arrowroot
30 g (1 oz/5 teaspoons) caster sugar
50 g (2 oz) elderberries, if desired

STUFFING: 30 g (1 oz/6 teaspoons) butter
6 shallots, finely chopped
155 ml (5 fl oz/²⁄₃ cup) gooseberry juice
30 g (1 oz/1¼ cups) chopped fresh mixed herbs
375 g (12 oz/6¼ cups) soft breadcrumbs
1 teaspoon salt
1 teaspoon ground black pepper

Preheat oven to 220C (425F/Gas 7). Remove giblets from goose; reserve liver. Use giblets to make stock. Prick goose skin all over. To make stuffing, melt butter in a pan, add shallots and liver; fry for 2 minutes. Stir in ½ gooseberry juice, herbs, all but 6 teaspoons of breadcrumbs and salt and pepper. Stuff neck end of goose; place remainder in body cavity. Cover goose with bacon; cook in oven for 45 minutes. Reduce oven to 190C (375F/Gas 5); cook for 1½ hours, pouring off excess fat during cooking.

Remove bacon, chop very finely; mix with remaining breadcrumbs. Brush goose with mustard; sprinkle with crumb mixture. Return to oven for a further 20-30 minutes until meat is tender. Place on a serving plate. Pour away excess fat, add 60 ml (2 fl oz/¼ cup) stock to roasting tin, mix with remaining gooseberry juice, add wine, gooseberries, arrowroot and sugar. Boil for 1 minute, stirring. Process until smooth. Strain sauce and stir in elderberries, if desired.

Serves 6-8.

SPICED HONEY GAMMON

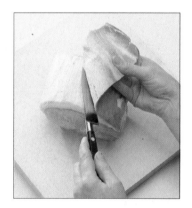

1.5 kg (3 lb) joint wood-smoked gammon
finely shredded peel and juice of 2 oranges
6 teaspoons clear honey
1 teaspoon ground mace
1 teaspoon grated fresh root ginger
125 g (4 oz) kumquats, sliced
6 teaspoons whole cloves
3 teaspoons cornflour

Soak gammon joint overnight in a bowl of cold water. Drain, transfer to a large saucepan and cover with fresh cold water. Bring to boil, cover and cook for 30 minutes. Drain and cool. Remove skin from gammon, leaving a layer of fat on surface of gammon.

Score fat on the surface of gammon into a lattice pattern with a sharp knife. Preheat oven to 190C (375F/Gas 5); place gammon in roasting tin. In a bowl, mix together orange peel, juice, honey, mace and ginger until evenly blended. Brush a little mixture over surface of gammon and bake in the oven for 30 minutes. Remove gammon from oven, brush surface with more orange mixture. Cover surface of gammon with kumquat slices, held in position with whole cloves.

Return to oven for a further 30-40 minutes until gammon is golden brown and tender. Remove and place on a serving dish. Keep warm. Add 185 ml (6 fl oz/¾ cup) water to roasting tin, stir to mix juices, then strain into a saucepan. Blend cornflour with remaining orange juice and honey mixture, add to pan, bring to boil and cook for 1 minute. Pour into a jug and serve with gammon. Garnish with remaining kumquat slices.

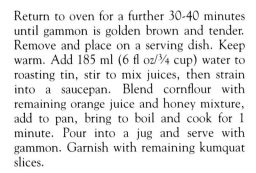

Serves 8.

TURKEY VEGETABLE STRUDEL

FRUIT PORK PILLOWS

9 leaves of filo or strudel pastry, thawed

SAUCE: 45 g (1½ oz/9 teaspoons) butter
45 g (1½ oz/¼ cup) plain flour
1 bay leaf
250 ml (8 fl oz/1 cup) milk
155 ml (5 fl oz/⅔ cup) single (light) cream
salt and ground black pepper

FILLING: 125 g (4 oz/½ cup) butter, melted
90 g (3 oz) leek, sliced
90 g (3 oz) fennel, thinly sliced
90 g (3 oz) button mushrooms, sliced
90 g (3 oz/1 cup) sweetcorn kernels
4 teaspoons chopped fresh parsley
250 g (8 oz/1 cup) diced, cooked turkey

Cover filo pastry with a damp cloth to prevent it drying. Preheat oven to 220C (425F/Gas 7). To make sauce, put butter, flour, bay leaf and milk in a saucepan. Bring to boil, whisking until thick. Cook gently for 2 minutes, then stir in cream and salt and pepper. To make filling, place 6 teaspoons of butter in a frying pan, add leek, fennel and mushrooms and fry gently for 2-3 minutes. Stir in sweetcorn, parsley and turkey. Mix with the sauce and leave until cold.

Lay 3 sheets of filo pastry flat on a tea towel, brushing between each sheet with melted butter. Spread with ⅓ of filling to within 2.5 cm (1 in) of edges, repeat twice more using remaining pastry and filling. Fold in all edges, roll up neatly into a roll with aid of tea towel and roll onto a greaseproof paper-lined baking sheet. Brush with remaining butter and cook in the oven for 20-25 minutes until golden brown. Serve hot, cut into slices.

Serves 6.

30 g (1 oz/6 teapoons) butter
2 tenderloins pork, cut into 8 pieces
125 g (4 oz/1 cup) dried apricots, chopped
9 teaspoons whipping cream, whipped
500 g (1 lb) puff pastry, thawed if frozen
125 g (4 oz/⅔ cup) fresh or canned cherries, stoned
  and halved
8 fresh sage leaves
salt and black pepper
a little beaten egg
cherries and sage leaves, to garnish

Preheat oven to 200C (400F/Gas 6). Line a baking sheet with non-stick paper. Melt butter in a frying pan. Fry pork for 1 minute.

Drain and cool pork. In a bowl, mix together apricots and cream. Cut pastry into 8 pieces, roll out one piece very thinly and trim to a neat square, measuring about 10 cm (4 in). Spread ⅛ apricot filling over centre, top with 4 cherry halves, a sage leaf and a piece of pork. Season to taste with salt and pepper.

Brush pastry edges with beaten egg, fold pastry over pork and seal edges well. Invert onto baking sheet and brush with egg to glaze. Repeat to make another 7 parcels. Roll out and cut pastry trimmings into holly leaves, berries and thin pastry strips and use to decorate each parcel. Glaze with egg and bake in the oven for 20-30 minutes until pastry is risen and golden brown. Serve hot, garnished with cherries and sage leaves.

Serves 8.

TURKEY RISOTTO

60 g (2 oz/¼ cup) butter
1 large onion, sliced
1 clove garlic, crushed
125 g (4 oz) button mushrooms, sliced
185 g (6 oz/1 cup) Italian risotto rice
1 teaspoon saffron strands
1 teaspoon salt
½ teaspoon ground black pepper
470 ml (15 fl oz/1¾ cups) turkey stock
155 ml (5 fl oz/⅔ cup) white wine
1 small red pepper (capsicum)
1 small yellow pepper (capsicum)
315 g (10 oz) cooked turkey
30 g (1 oz/6 teaspoons) grated Gruyère cheese
3 teaspoons chopped fresh parsley

Melt butter in a flameproof dish or saucepan, add onion, garlic and mushrooms and cook for 2 minutes until tender. Stir in rice and cook for a further 2 minutes. Add saffron, salt, pepper, stock and wine, bring to boil, stirring, then cover and cook very gently for 15 minutes. Grill red and yellow peppers (capsicums) until skin has charred and peppers (capsicums) are tender. Remove stalks, seeds and skin and cut peppers (capsicums) into fine strips. Cut turkey into bite-sized pieces.

Add turkey and peppers (capsicums) to risotto, stir carefully to distribute ingredients, then cover and cook for a further 5 minutes until rice is tender and mixture is creamy, but not dry. Serve risotto in the flameproof dish or arrange on a warmed serving plate. Sprinkle with cheese and parsley and serve hot.

Serves 4-6.

CLEMENTINE DUCK

2.5 kg (5 lb) oven-ready duck with giblets
salt
30 g (1 oz/6 teaspoons) butter
3 shallots, finely chopped
315 ml (10 fl oz/1¼ cups) rosé wine
½ teaspoon ground black pepper
1 teaspoon wholegrain mustard
3 teaspoons chopped fresh oregano
finely grated peel and juice of 2 clementines
6 teaspoons redcurrant jelly
90 g (3 oz/¾ cup) redcurrants, thawed
1 egg, beaten
90 g (3 oz/1½ cups) soft white breadcrumbs
clementine wedges, redcurrants and oregano sprigs, to garnish

Preheat oven to 220C (425F/Gas 7). Remove duck giblets; reserve liver and chop. Prick skin all over with a fork and rub with salt. Place duck in a roasting tin. Cook in oven for 45 minutes until golden; cool for 15 minutes. Remove duck and strain fat from roasting tin. Melt butter in a pan, add shallots and liver and fry quickly, stirring, until shallots are tender. Add wine, salt, pepper and mustard; boil for 5 minutes. Mix into roasting tin; strain back into pan. Add the oregano, the grated clementine peel and juice and redcurrant jelly.

Cut off leg and wing joints from duck. Cut breast into thin slices and arrange in a warm ovenproof dish. Pour over sauce, add redcurrants, cover dish; keep warm. Brush duck joints with egg, coat with breadcrumbs and arrange in a roasting tin. Return to oven for 20-30 minutes until golden brown. Arrange on a serving dish with breast meat and sauce. Garnish with clementine wedges, redcurrants and oregano sprigs.

Serves 4.

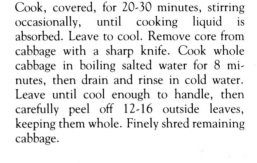

BEEF-STUFFED CABBAGE

2 onions
5 tablespoons vegetable oil
3 cloves garlic, crushed
2 fresh green chillies, seeded and chopped
7.5 cm (3 in) piece fresh root ginger, grated
500 g (1 lb) lean minced beef
¼ teaspoon turmeric
¼ teaspoon Garam Masala
1 savoy cabbage
440 g (14 oz) can chopped tomatoes
6 teaspoons lemon juice
salt and pepper
lemon or lime slices, to garnish

Chop 1 onion and slice the other.

Heat 2 tablespoons oil in a heavy-based pan, add chopped onion and cook over a medium heat, stirring, for about 8 minutes, until soft and golden brown. Add garlic, chillies and one-third of the ginger and cook for 1 minute, then remove with a slotted spoon and set aside.

Add beef to pan and cook, stirring, until browned and well broken up. Stir in turmeric and garam masala and cook for 1 minute, then add onion mixture.

Cook, covered, for 20-30 minutes, stirring occasionally, until cooking liquid is absorbed. Leave to cool. Remove core from cabbage with a sharp knife. Cook whole cabbage in boiling salted water for 8 minutes, then drain and rinse in cold water. Leave until cool enough to handle, then carefully peel off 12-16 outside leaves, keeping them whole. Finely shred remaining cabbage.

To make sauce, heat remaining oil in a heavy-based pan, add sliced onion and cook, stirring frequently, for 5 minutes or until soft but not brown. Add shredded cabbage, tomatoes, remaining ginger, lemon juice and 155ml (5 fl oz/⅔ cup) water. Season with salt and pepper. Bring to the boil, then simmer, uncovered, for 5 minutes.

Preheat oven to 190C (375F/Gas 5). Put about 2 tablespoons mince mixture on each cabbage leaf, fold sides in and roll up neatly. Pour a little sauce into base of an ovenproof casserole, add cabbage rolls and pour over remaining sauce. Cover and cook for 40-50 minutes, until cabbage is tender. Serve hot, garnished with lemon or lime slices.

Serves 4.

APPLE & ELDERFLOWER PORK

1.25 kg (2½ lb) loin of pork, boned

4 teaspoons plain flour

MARINADE:

315 ml (10 fl oz/1¼ cups) elderflower wine

2 heads of elderflowers

4 teaspoons clear honey

6 teaspoons almond oil

3 fresh bay leaves

STUFFING:

250 g (8 oz/2 cups) peeled and chopped cooking apples

6 teaspoons elderflower wine

1 teaspoon clear honey

3 teaspoons snipped fresh chives

60 g (2 oz/½ cup) white breadcrumbs

GARNISH:

elderflowers

apple slices dipped in lemon juice

Trim any excess fat from meat and remove rind, leaving a thin layer of fat. Score to make a lattice pattern. Mix marinade ingredients together.

Immerse pork in marinade. Cover and leave in cool place for 4 hours.

Preheat oven to 190C (375F/Gas 5). To make stuffing, put apples, wine and honey in a pan, bring to boil and cook, stirring, until liquid has been absorbed. Stir in chives and breadcrumbs. Cool.

Remove meat from marinade and pat dry. Spread stuffing over centre, roll up and tie with string. Place in roasting tin, brush with marinade and cook for 1 hour, basting.

Remove meat from tin, stir flour into juices and add remaining marinade and 155 ml (5 fl oz/⅔ cup) water. Bring to boil, and cook for 2 minutes. Strain into a bowl.

Remove string, then cut meat into thin slices. Pour some of the sauce over a serving plate. Arrange pork slices on top and garnish.

Serves 6.

BEEF IN WINE

750 g (1½ lb) thick rib braising steak, well trimmed and cubed

30 g (1 oz/6 teaspoons) butter

185 g (6 oz/2 cups) button mushrooms

155 ml (5 fl oz/⅔ cup) beef stock

30 g (1 oz/¼ cup) plain flour

3 teaspoons tomato purée (paste)

oregano and winter savory sprigs, to garnish

MARINADE:

155 ml (5 fl oz/⅔ cup) red wine

½ cucumber, thinly sliced

1 red onion, thinly sliced

3 teaspoons chopped fresh oregano

3 teaspoons chopped fresh winter savory

1 clove garlic

2 teaspoons brown sugar

½ teaspoon salt

½ teaspoon black pepper

To make marinade, mix red wine, cucumber, onion, oregano, winter savory, garlic, sugar, salt and pepper together in a casserole. Add meat and stir well. Cover and leave in cool place for 4 hours.

Preheat oven to 180C (350F/Gas 4). Strain marinade into a bowl, remove cucumber slices and place on a plate.

Melt butter in frying pan, add mushrooms, meat, onion and herbs in sieve and fry quickly to brown meat. Add marinade and stock and bring to the boil, then return to casserole.

Cover and cook for 2 hours, until tender. Mix together flour and tomato purée (paste) and stir into casserole to thicken gravy. Add the cucumber slices. Serve garnished with oregano and winter savory.

Serves 4-6.

HORSERADISH STEAK

500 g (1 lb) rump steak, cut into thin strips

30 g (1 oz/6 teaspoons) butter

6 teaspoons sherry

thyme sprigs, to garnish

MARINADE:

4 teaspoons horseradish sauce

4 teaspoons strained Greek yogurt

2 teaspoons paprika

3 teaspoons chopped fresh thyme

½ teaspoon salt

½ teaspoon black pepper

To make marinade, mix horseradish, yogurt, paprika, thyme, salt and pepper together, stirring until well blended. Add meat and stir to coat evenly. Cover with plastic wrap and leave in a cool place for 1 hour.

Melt butter in frying pan. Remove steak from marinade using a slotted spoon, add to frying pan and cook quickly for 1 minute. Lift strips of steak out and place on a serving dish.

Stir remaining marinade and sherry into pan and bring to the boil, stirring well. Pour over steak on serving dish and garnish with a few sprigs of fresh thyme.

Serves 4.

JUNIPER LAMB

625 g (1¼ lb) loin of lamb, well trimmed and boned

4 teaspoons plain flour

MARINADE:

250 ml (8 fl oz/1 cup) rosé wine

4 teaspoons juniper berries, crushed

2 teaspoons Angostura bitters

2 bay leaves

½ teaspoon salt

½ teaspoon black pepper

STUFFING:

60 g (2 oz/1 cup) fresh white breadcrumbs

60 g (2 oz) pre-soaked dried apricots

2 teaspoons lemon juice

2 teaspoons finely grated lemon peel

2 teaspoons chopped fresh rosemary

GARNISH:

lemon wedges

6 apricots

rosemary sprigs

To make marinade, mix all ingredients together, add lamb and turn to coat evenly. Cover and leave in a cool place for 4 hours or overnight.

Preheat oven to 190C (375F/Gas 5). To make stuffing, process bread, apricots, lemon juice, peel and rosemary in a food processor.

Remove lamb from marinade and pat dry. Spread stuffing over centre of meat, roll up, and tie securely in several places. Place in roasting tin, brush well with marinade and cook for 45-50 minutes, basting with marinade if necessary. Place meat on a serving plate; keep warm.

Stir flour into tin, add remaining marinade and bring to the boil, stirring: add a little water if too thick. Strain into serving bowl.

Remove string from meat, cut meat into thin slices and pour some of sauce over a serving plate. Arrange lamb in centre and garnish.

Serves 4-6.

GAMMON STEAKS

4 gammon steaks, about 625 g (1¼ lb) in weight
MARINADE:
2 teaspoons light soy sauce
3 teaspoons sherry vinegar
6 teaspoons groundnut oil
3 teaspoons clear honey
3 teaspoons chopped fresh rosemary
6 whole cloves
2.5 cm (1 in) stick cinnamon
½ teaspoon ground black pepper
1 cooking apple, peeled and grated
GARNISH:
rosemary sprigs
apple slices
3 teaspoons lemon juice

Soak gammon steaks in cold water for several hours or overnight. Drain and dry on kitchen paper, then place in a shallow dish.

To make marinade, mix soy sauce, vinegar, groundnut oil, honey, rosemary, cloves, cinnamon, pepper and apple together, stirring well.

Pour marinade over gammon steaks and turn to coat evenly. Cover with plastic wrap and leave in a cool place for 1 hour.

Meanwhile, prepare barbecue or preheat grill to hot. Cook gammon for 3-5 minutes, turning once and brushing with extra marinade. Arrange on a warmed serving dish and serve garnished with sprigs of rosemary and the apple slices tossed in lemon juice.

Serves 4.

PEPPERCORN STEAKS

4 fillets of steak, about 500 g (1 lb)
30 g (1 oz/6 teaspoons) butter
3 teaspoons double (thick) cream
MARINADE:
3 teaspoons wholegrain mustard
2 teaspoons green peppercorns, crushed
2 teaspoons pink peppercorns, crushed
3 teaspoons tomato purée (paste)
½ teaspoon salt
2 teaspoons chopped fresh marjoram
2 teaspoons chopped fresh oregano
2 teaspoons chopped fresh basil
GARNISH:
pink and green peppercorns
marjoram and oregano sprigs
basil leaves

To make marinade, mix mustard, the green and pink peppercorns, tomato purée (paste), salt, marjoram, oregano and basil together, stirring until well mixed.

Spread marinade evenly over each fillet steak to coat. Place on a plate, cover with plastic wrap and leave in a cool place for 1 hour or until ready to cook.

Melt butter in frying pan, add fillet steaks and cook quickly to seal surfaces, then turn and cook undersides. Continue cooking for 3-5 minutes according to desired degree of doneness.

Arrange each steak on a warmed serving plate and keep warm. Stir cream into juices in frying pan and bring to the boil.

Pour a little sauce over each steak, then serve garnished with a few pink and green peppercorns, sprigs of oregano and fresh marjoram and basil leaves.

Serves 4.

PEPPERED PORK

4 pork escalopes, about 500g (1 lb)

orange slices and ginger mint sprigs, to garnish

MARINADE:

1 small yellow pepper (capsicum)

1 small orange pepper (capsicum)

1 clove garlic

4 teaspoons olive oil

2 teaspoons grated orange peel

6 teaspoons freshly squeezed orange juice

2 teaspoons clear honey

6 teaspoons chopped fresh ginger mint

Peheat oven to 200C (400F/Gas 6). To make marinade, place peppers (capsicums) in an oven-proof dish and bake for 10-15 minutes, until skin has burnt and peels off easily. Cool slightly, then peel and remove stalks and seeds. Place in a food processor fitted with a metal blade and process until smooth. Add garlic, oil, orange peel and juice, honey and chopped ginger mint and process again.

Arrange pork in an ovenproof dish, pour over pepper marinade and turn pork to coat evenly. Cover with plastic wrap and leave in a cool place for 30 minutes.

Cook for 15 minutes, until cooked through. Arrange on a warmed serving dish and garnish with orange slice and mint sprigs.

Serves 4.

POMEGRANATE & LIME LAMB

4 double lamb chops, about 625 g (1¼ lb)

redcurrant strands and thyme sprigs, to garnish

MARINADE:

2 pomegranates, peeled

finely grated peel of 1 lime

3 teaspoons freshly squeezed lime juice

3 teaspoons redcurrant jelly

3 teaspoons chopped fresh thyme

¼ teaspoon salt

½ teaspoon black pepper

SAUCE:

30 g (1 oz/6 teaspoons) butter

1 small red onion, thinly sliced

15 g (½ oz/6 teaspoons) plain flour

To make marinade, scrape pome-granate seeds into a sieve over a bowl, reserving a few for garnish. Press remainder through sieve with a wooden spoon to extract juice.

Put 4 teaspoons juice in another bowl with all remaining marinade ingredients.

Put chops in a shallow dish and brush each with marinade to coat evenly. Cover with plastic wrap and leave for 1 hour in a cool place.

Preheat a moderately hot grill. Grill chops for 5-8 minutes on each side, turning once and brushing with marinade. Keep warm.

Melt butter in saucepan, add onion and cook gently for 1-2 minutes, until tender. Stir in flour and cook for 1 minute, stirring, then remove saucepan from heat. Make up remaining pomegranate juice to 250 ml (8 fl oz/1 cup) with juices from the grill pan and water. Stir into saucepan, bring to the boil, stirring, and cook 2 minutes.

Pour a little sauce onto a warmed serving plate, arrange chops on top and garnish with redcurrant strands, reserved seeds and thyme sprigs.

Serves 4.

PORK WITH HERBS

1 pork tenderloin, about 500 g (1 lb), well trimmed
4 teaspoons plain flour
4 teaspoons single (light) cream
oregano sprigs and sage leaves, to garnish
MARINADE:
6 teaspoons olive oil
3 teaspoons Madeira
½ teaspoon salt
½ teaspoon black pepper
1 teaspoon Dijon wholegrain mustard
1 teaspoon caster sugar
3 teaspoons grated onion
3 teaspoons chopped fresh sage
3 teaspoons chopped fresh oregano

To make marinade, mix oil, Madeira, salt, pepper, mustard, sugar, onion, sage and oregano together, stirring until well blended.

Pour over pork tenderloin in a shallow ovenproof bowl and turn to coat evenly. Cover with plastic wrap and leave in a cool place for 2-3 hours.

Preheat oven to 220C (425F/Gas 7). Cook pork for 15 minutes, basting with marinade if necessary, until tender and cooked through. Place on a plate and keep warm.

Stir flour into remaining marinade in dish and pour into a saucepan. Bring to the boil and cook for 2 minutes, adding a little water if too thick. Remove from heat and stir in cream.

Slice the pork into 1 cm (½ in) slices and pour sauce on to a serving plate. Arrange sliced pork on top and garnish with oregano and sage.

Serves 4.

ROSY ROASTED GAMMON

1.25-1.5 kg (2½-3 lb) piece gammon
3 teaspoons whole cloves
2 teaspoons arrowroot
6 teaspoons redcurrant jelly
redcurrant strands and oregano sprigs, to garnish
MARINADE:
250 g (8 oz/2 cups) redcurrants
6 teaspoons light soft brown sugar
9 teaspoons chopped fresh oregano
3 teaspoons olive oil

Soak gammon joint in cold water for several hours or overnight. Drain and rinse in fresh water, then place in a large saucepan, cover with cold water; bring to the boil.

Cover and simmer for 30 minutes. Remove gammon from saucepan and cool, then peel off rind.

To make marinade, put redcurrants in a sieve over a bowl and press through juice using a wooden spoon. Stir in sugar, oregano and oil and pour into a large bowl. Add gammon joint and turn in marinade to coat. Cover with plastic wrap and leave in a cool place for 1 hour.

Preheat oven to 190C (375F/Gas 5). Using a sharp knife, score fat on gammon into a lattice pattern. Press cloves into each diamond shape and brush with marinade.

Place in a roasting tin and cook for 45-50 minutes, brushing with extra marinade. Cover with foil if the surface becomes too brown.

Place gammon on a serving plate and keep warm. Blend arrowroot and 155 ml (5 fl oz/⅔ cup) water together, add to roasting tin with marinade and stir well to mix with juices. Strain into a saucepan, add redcurrant jelly, then bring to the boil, stirring, and cook for 1 minute. Pour around gammon and garnish.

Serves 4-6.

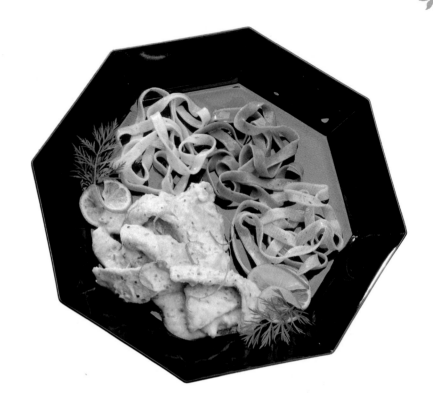

SAFFRON LAMB CUTLETS

8 lamb cutlets, about 625 g (1¼ lb)

8 sheets filo pastry, thawed if frozen

60 g (2 oz/¼ cup) butter, melted

rosemary sprigs and orange slices, to garnish

MARINADE:

155 ml (5 fl oz/⅔ cup) thick sour cream

2 teaspoons finely grated orange peel

3 teaspoons freshly squeezed orange juice

½ teaspoon saffron threads or a good pinch powdered saffron

2 teaspoons chopped fresh rosemary

¼ teaspoon salt

¼ teaspoon black pepper

Trim away any excess fat from each cutlet and strip off fat and skin from each bone above eye of meat, leaving bones clean.

To make marinade, mix sour cream, orange peel and juice, saffron, rosemary, salt and pepper together, stirring until blended.

Place cutlets in a dish and spread marinade over both sides of the meat. Cover with foil and leave in a cool place for 3-4 hours.

Preheat oven to 230C (450F/Gas 8). Cover baking sheet with foil, arrange cutlets a little apart and cook at the top of oven for 5-8 minutes, until marinade has set and chop is tinged with brown. Cool cutlets for 15 minutes.

Brush each piece of filo pastry with butter and fold in half. Wrap each cutlet in pastry, leaving the bone uncovered.

Arrange cutlets on a buttered baking sheet, brush with remaining butter and return to oven for 10-12 minutes, until pastry is crisp and golden brown.

Arrange on a warmed serving dish garnished with sprigs of rosemary and orange slices.

Serves 4.

SPICED GAMMON

625 g (1¼ lb) gammon

90 g (3 oz) creamed coconut

6 teaspoons mango chutney

juice of 1 lime

9 teaspoons sour cream

lime slices and parsley sprigs, to garnish

MARINADE:

2 teaspoons cumin seeds, toasted

1 teaspoon allspice berries

½ teaspoon mustard seeds

½ teaspoon white peppercorns

½ teaspoon black peppercorns

2 teaspoons grated lime peel

30 g (1 oz/6 teaspoons) butter, melted

Soak gammon in cold water for several hours or overnight. Drain and rinse in fresh water, then place in large saucepan, cover with water and bring to the boil.

Cover and simmer for 30 minutes. Remove gammon from saucepan and cool, then cut into thin strips.

To make marinade, mix cumin seeds, allspice, mustard seeds and peppercorns together in a pestle and mortar. Crush finely, then add lime peel and butter, working until the butter paste is well blended and smooth.

Rub marinade into gammon strips and place in a bowl. Cover with plastic wrap and leave in cool place for 2-3 hours.

Heat a non-stick frying pan, add meat and fry quickly for 2-3 minutes. Stir in coconut, chutney and lime juice, bring to the boil and cook for 2-3 minutes.

Remove pan from heat and stir in sour cream. Pour gammon mixture into a warmed serving dish and serve garnished with lime slices and parsley sprigs.

Serves 4.

SPICED SKEWERED LAMB

2 lamb neck fillets, about 500 g (1 lb), trimmed and cut into 7.5 cm (3 in) long strips

MARINADE:

1 teaspoon ground allspice

1 teaspoon grated fresh root ginger

3 teaspoons clear honey

6 teaspoons sherry vinegar

90 ml (3 fl oz/⅓ cup) apple juice

6 teaspoons chopped fresh mint

4 teaspoons olive oil

GARNISH:

fresh mint leaves

8 apple wedges

3 teaspoons lemon juice

8 lemon wedges

To make marinade, mix allspice, ginger, honey, sherry vinegar, apple juice, mint and oil together, stirring until evenly blended.

Add lamb strips and turn in marinade to coat each piece evenly. Cover with plastic wrap and leave in a cool place for 2-3 hours. Meanwhile, soak 8 fine wooden barbecue skewers in cold water. Prepare barbecue or preheat grill.

Thread several pieces of lamb onto each skewer and barbecue or grill for 2-3 minutes, turning once and brushing with more marinade if necessary.

Arrange lamb on a warmed serving plate, garnished with fresh mint leaves, wedges of apple tossed in lemon juice and lemon wedges.

Put remaining marinade in a saucepan, bring to the boil and pour into a dish. Serve with the lamb.

Serves 4.

SWEET & SOUR SPARE RIBS

12 pork spare ribs, about 750 g (1½ lb), trimmed

fresh herbs, to garnish

MARINADE:

3 teaspoons soy sauce

2 teaspoons clear honey

3 teaspoons dry sherry

9 teaspoons tomato purée (paste)

1 clove garlic, crushed

1 small chilli, seeded and chopped

2 teaspoons grated fresh root ginger

2.5 cm (1 in) cinnamon stick

6 cloves

½ teaspoon yellow mustard seeds

½ teaspoon salt

1 teaspoon black peppercorns

To make marinade, mix soy sauce, honey, sherry, tomato purée (paste),

garlic, chilli and ginger together. In a pestle and mortar, crush the cinnamon, cloves, mustard seeds, salt and peppercorns until ground and blended. Stir the ground spice mixture into the marinade until evenly blended.

Pour marinade over spare ribs and turn to coat evenly. Cover with plastic wrap and leave in a cool place for 2-3 hours.

Meanwhile, prepare barbecue or preheat grill. Cook spare ribs for 5-8 minutes, until crisp, turning once and brushing with more marinade if necessary. Serve garnished with fresh herbs.

Serves 4.

CHICKEN BITES

4 chicken breasts (fillets), about 750 g (1½ lb), cut into thin strips
24 kumquats
winter savory, oregano sprigs and sliced kumquats, to garnish
MARINADE:
155 g (5 oz/⅔ cup) strained Greek yogurt
2 teaspoons tomato purée (paste)
2 teaspoons Worcestershire sauce
6 teaspoons mango chutney
½ teaspoon salt
½ teaspoon black pepper
4 teaspoons chopped fresh oregano
4 teaspoons chopped fresh winter savory

Soak 12 wooden skewers in water.

To make marinade, mix yogurt, tomato purée (paste), Worcestershire sauce, chutney, salt, pepper and chopped oregano and winter savory together until well blended. Add chicken, stir to coat evenly and leave in cool place for 3 hours.

Meanwhile, prepare barbecue or preheat grill. Thread alternate slices of kumquat and pieces of chicken onto each kebab skewer.

Cook chicken bites for 5-8 minutes, turning once and brushing with marinade if necessary.

Serve hot, garnished with sprigs of winter savory, oregano and sliced kumquats.

Serves 4.

CRISPY GRAPEFRUIT CHICKEN

8 chicken thighs, about 1.25 kg (2 lb)
grapefruit segments and rosemary sprigs, to garnish
MARINADE:
3 teaspoons chopped fresh rosemary
3 teaspoons clear honey
60 ml (2 fl oz/¼ cup) olive oil
¾ teaspoon cayenne pepper
2 teaspoons finely grated grapefruit peel
6 teaspoons freshly squeezed grapefruit juice

To make marinade, mix rosemary, honey, olive oil, cayenne, grapefruit peel and juice together until well blended.

Place chicken thighs in a shallow ovenproof dish, pour over marinade and turn chicken until evenly coated. Cover with plastic wrap and leave to marinate in a cool place for 3-4 hours.

Preheat oven to 220C (425F/Gas 7), or prepare a barbecue. Cook chicken for 20-25 minutes, until golden brown and skin is crisp, basting with marinade if necessary.

Arrange chicken on a serving plate and garnish with grapefruit segments and rosemary sprigs.

Serves 4.

CURRIED DRUMSTICKS

| 8 chicken drumsticks |
| MARINADE: |
| 1 teaspoon mild curry paste |
| 2 teaspoons finely grated lime peel |
| 3 teaspoons freshly squeezed lime juice |
| 30 g (1 oz/4 teaspoons) creamed coconut |
| 1 teaspoon clear honey |
| ½ teaspoon salt |
| ½ teaspoon black pepper |
| COATING: |
| 60 g (2 oz/¼ cup) butter, softened |
| 1 clove garlic, crushed |
| 3 teaspoons chopped fresh coriander |
| 45 g (1½ oz/⅓ cup) fresh white breadcrumbs |

Wipe chicken drumsticks with absorbent kitchen paper.

To make marinade, mix curry paste, lime peel and juice, coconut,

honey, salt and pepper together, stirring to form a paste.

Spread marinade evenly over each drumstick to coat. Place on a plate, cover with foil and leave in a cool place for 2 hours.

Preheat oven to 200C (400F/Gas 6). Blend together butter, garlic and coriander until soft and smooth. Place in an ovenproof dish and melt in oven.

Coat each drumstick evenly with breadcrumbs, then roll in butter mixture. Return to oven and cook for 30 minutes, until golden brown and juices run clear when drumsticks are pierced with tip of knife. Serve with a mixed salad.

Makes 8.

DEVILLED TURKEY WINGS

| 4 turkey wings |
| 90 g (3 oz/⅓ cup) butter, melted |
| watercress sprigs and tomato wedges, to garnish |
| MARINADE: |
| 2 teaspoons ground ginger |
| 2 teaspoons white pepper |
| 2 teaspoons dry mustard |
| 1 teaspoon salt |
| 1 teaspoon curry powder |
| 3 teaspoons soft brown sugar |
| SAUCE: |
| 60 ml (2 fl oz/¼ cup) tomato sauce |
| 6 teaspoons Worcestershire sauce |
| 3 teaspoons soy sauce |
| 6 teaspoons mango chutney |

To make marinade, mix ginger, pepper, mustard, salt, curry powder and sugar together in a polythene bag. Shake until well mixed.

Place 1 turkey wing in the bag at a time and shake well to coat evenly with marinade. Place on a plate, cover with plastic wrap and leave in a cool place for 1 hour.

Preheat grill to moderate. Brush each turkey wing generously with butter, then grill for 10-12 minutes, turning frequently, until golden brown and turkey is cooked through. Arrange on a serving plate and keep warm.

To make the sauce, add tomato, Worcestershire and soy sauces to grill pan with chutney. Stir well, cooking under grill until sauce bubbles. Pour over turkey wings and garnish with watercress sprigs and tomato wedges.

Serves 4.

CRANBERRY & ORANGE DUCK

1 duck, about 2 kg (4 lb), cut into 4 joints
2 teaspoons arrowroot
2 teaspoons orange juice
MARINADE:
125 g (4 oz/1 cup) cranberries
8 teaspoons clear honey
2 teaspoons finely grated orange peel
6 teaspoons freshly squeezed orange juice
155 ml (5 fl oz/⅔ cup) rosé wine
4 teaspoons chopped fresh sage
½ teaspoon each salt and black pepper
GARNISH:
orange slices
4 teaspoons cranberries
fresh sage leaves

Trim off excess fat and skin from duck joints to neaten.

To make marinade, place cranberries and honey in a small saucepan with 155 ml (5 fl oz/⅔ cup) water and boil. Cover and cook for 3 or 4 minutes, until tender. Press through a sieve to purée. Stir in remaining marinade ingredients.

Add duck joints to marinade and turn to coat evenly. Cover with plastic wrap and leave in a cool place for 4 hours or overnight.

Preheat oven to 220C (425F/Gas 7). Remove duck joints from marinade and arrange in an ovenproof dish. Cook for 45 minutes. Reduce temperature to 190C (375F/Gas 5). Pour marinade over duck, cover and cook for 40 minutes, or until duck is cooked and juices run clear when pierced with tip of knife. Place on a serving plate and keep warm.

Blend arrowroot and orange juice in a small pan. Pour off most of fat from marinade, add marinade to arrowroot mixture. Bring to boil, stirring, then cook gently 1 minute, until thick and clear. Pour sauce over duck, then garnish.

Serves 4.

GOLDEN TURKEY

4 turkey steaks, about 500 g (1 lb)
fresh coriander leaves and lime wedges, to garnish
MARINADE:
12 cardamom pods
2 teaspoons coriander seeds
½ teaspoon yellow mustard seeds
1 clove garlic, crushed
3 teaspoons grated lime peel
½ teaspoon salt
½ teaspoon black pepper
COATING:
1 clove garlic, crushed
60 g (2 oz/¼ cup) butter
45 g (1½ oz/⅓ cup) plain potato crisps, crushed

To make marinade, remove seeds from cardamom pods and place in a pestle and mortar with coriander and mustard seeds. Crush until finely blended. Add garlic, lime peel, salt and pepper; mix well.

Cut a small slit in each turkey steak to make a pocket.

Spread marinade mixture over turkey steaks, rubbing well into the flesh. Place in dish, cover with plastic wrap and leave in a cool place for 2-3 hours.

Preheat oven to 220C (425F/Gas 7). Blend together remaining garlic and butter, beating well until smooth and soft. Spread each turkey steak evenly with half garlic butter, and fill each cavity with remainder.

Coat turkey steaks evenly in crushed crisps and arrange in a small roasting tin, cavity side uppermost. Cook for 15 minutes, until golden brown and crisp and cooked through.

Arrange on a serving plate and garnish with fresh coriander leaves and lime wedges.

Serves 4.

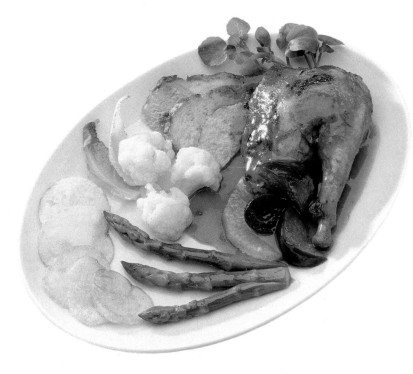

TURKEY STROGANOFF

| 3 turkey breast (fillets), about 750g (1½ lb), cut into thin slices |
| 30 g (1 oz/6 teaspoons) butter |
| 3 teaspoons olive oil |
| 185 g (6 oz) button mushrooms |
| 3 teaspoons lemon juice |
| 155 ml (5 fl oz/⅔ cup) pineapple juice |
| 155 ml (5 fl oz/⅔ cup) chicken stock |
| 155 ml (5 fl oz/⅔ cup) single (light) cream |
| 1 egg yolk |
| flesh from ½ pineapple, chopped |
| 30 g (1 oz/½ cup) flaked almonds, toasted, and parsley sprigs, to garnish |
| MARINADE: |
| 6 teaspoons plain flour |
| ½ teaspoon ground cloves |
| 1 teaspoon grated nutmeg |
| ½ teaspoon salt |
| ½ teaspoon black pepper |
| 2 teaspoons grated lemon peel |

To make marinade, mix flour, cloves, nutmeg, salt, pepper and lemon peel together in a dish.

Add turkey pieces and turn in mixture to coat evenly. Cover with plastic wrap and a leave in a cool place for 1 hour.

Melt butter and oil in a frying pan. Add turkey and mushrooms and cook quickly, stirring occasionally. Stir in lemon and pineapple juices and stock and bring to the boil, then cover the pan and cook for 5 minutes.

Beat together cream and egg yolk, then stir cream into turkey and mushroom mixture and immediately remove from the heat.

Stir in half pineapple and pour mixture into a warmed serving dish. Garnish with the remaining chopped pineapple, flaked almonds and sprigs of parsley.

Serves 4.

PHEASANT IN MADEIRA

| 1 oven-ready pheasant |
| 30 g (1 oz/6 teaspoons) butter |
| 4 teaspoons plain flour |
| 6 teaspoons single (light) cream |
| MARINADE: |
| 1 teaspoon clear honey |
| 2 teaspoons finely grated grapefruit peel |
| 6 teaspoons chopped fresh purple basil |
| 6 teaspoons snipped fresh chives |
| 1 teaspoon dry mustard |
| ½ teaspoon salt |
| ½ teaspoon black pepper |
| 155 ml (5 fl oz/⅔ cup) Madeira |
| 6 teaspoons olive oil |
| 4 figs, cut into quarters |
| 125 g (4 oz/1 cup) cherries, stoned |
| GARNISH: |
| 1 fresh fig, sliced |
| 8 cherries |
| grapefruit segments |
| watercress sprigs |

Cut pheasant into 4 joints, trim off excess skin; remove wing bones.

To make marinade, mix honey, grapefruit peel, basil, chives, mustard, salt, pepper, Madeira and oil together, then add fruit.

Add joints to marinade turning to coat. Cover with plastic wrap and leave in a cool place for 4 hours.

Preheat oven to 180C (350F/Gas 4). Melt butter in a frying pan, take joints out of marinade and fry quickly to brown. Add marinade, bring to the boil and pour into casserole dish. Cook for 1 hour or until pheasant is tender and juices run clear when pricked with knife.

Arrange pheasant joints on a warmed serving dish and keep warm. Skim fat off marinade. Blend flour and cream, add to marinade and bring to boil, stirring, until thick. Cook gently for 2 minutes, pour over pheasant, then garnish.

Serves 4.

POUSSIN PROVENÇAL

2 poussin, halved
1 red pepper (capsicum)
4 tomatoes, skinned, seeded and sliced
fresh basil leaves, to garnish
MARINADE:
10 stoned olives, halved
5 anchovy fillets, well drained and chopped
9 teaspoons olive oil
9 teaspoons sweet sherry
1 clove garlic, crushed
½ teaspoon black pepper
6 teaspoons chopped fresh basil

To make marinade, mix olives, anchovies, oil, sherry, garlic, pepper and basil together, stirring until well mixed. Add poussin and turn in marinade to coat evenly. Cover with plastic wrap and leave in a cool place for 4 hours.

Preheat oven to 220C (425F/Gas 7). Place pepper (capsicum) on a baking sheet, place in oven and cook until skin is burnt and flesh is tender. Remove from oven and set aside to cool.

Lift poussin joints out of marinade and arrange in an ovenproof dish, spooning a little marinade over each.

Cook for 30-40 minutes, until golden brown, crisp and juices run clear when pricked with the tip of a knife. Keep warm.

Skin pepper (capsicum), cut into strips and place in a saucepan with tomatoes and remaining marinade. Bring to the boil, then cook gently for 5 minutes, stirring occasionally.

Pour the mixture into a warmed serving dish, arrange the poussin joints on top and garnish the dish with basil leaves.

Serves 4.

STUFFED QUAIL IN PORT

4 oven-ready quails
fresh herb sprigs, to garnish
MARINADE:
90 ml (3 fl oz/⅓ cup) ruby port
6 teaspoons olive oil
3 teaspoons chopped fresh thyme
3 teaspoons chopped fresh oregano
3 teaspoons chopped fresh winter savory
1 clove garlic, crushed
½ teaspoon each salt and pepper
STUFFING:
30 g (1 oz) shallots
185 g (6 oz) button mushrooms
3 teaspoons chopped fresh parsley
125 g (4 oz) smoked streaky bacon, rinded and chopped

Cut feet and wing tips off each quail. Using kitchen scissors, split quails lengthwise, cutting through one side of backbone from neck to tail. Lay quails flat on a board with breast side uppermost and press to flatten, breaking backbone.

Make a slit between legs through flap of skin, then insert legs and pull through to secure. Loosen skin at breast end of bird for stuffing.

Mix marinade ingredients together, add quails and turn to coat. Cover and leave in a cool place 4 hours. To make stuffing, finely chop shallots, mushrooms and parsley. Add ½ teaspoon salt and pepper.

Heat a frying pan, and fry bacon until fat runs. Add mushroom mixture and fry until dry. Cool. Meanwhile, preheat grill.

Remove quail from marinade and insert stuffing under skin. Arrange on grill rack; brush with marinade. Cook for 10 minutes, turning once and basting with more marinade if necessary.

Arrange on a warmed serving dish and garnish with herbs.

Serves 4.

| 125 g (4 oz/1 cup) plain flour |
| pinch of salt |
| 2 eggs |
| 315 ml (10 fl oz/1¼ cups) milk |
| 3 teaspoons butter, melted |
| vegetable oil or lard for cooking |
| TO SERVE: lemon juice and sugar, or warmed jam |

Sift flour and salt into a bowl. Make a well in centre and add eggs and a little milk. Beat, working in all flour. Beat in remaining milk and butter.

Heat a little vegetable oil or lard in a 17.5 cm (7 in) crêpe pan, barely covering the base. Pour in 2–3 tablespoons batter, tilting the pan so the batter covers the base thinly and evenly. Cook over high heat for about 1 minute, until lightly browned underneath.

Turn crêpe with a palette knife and cook other side for about 30 seconds. Remove from pan and keep warm, then continue until all the batter is used. Serve with lemon juice and sugar, with warmed jam or savoury or sweet toppings or fillings.

Makes 8.

CHEESY ANCHOVY CRÊPES

| eight 17.5 cm (7 in) crêpes |
| 90 g (3 oz) can anchovies, drained |
| 125 g (4 oz) Gruyère cheese, cut into thin strips, plus extra, grated, to garnish |
| 155 ml (5 fl oz/⅔ cup) thick sour cream |
| 1 tablespoon lemon juice |
| salt and pepper |
| 1 tablespoon chopped fresh parsley |

Keep crêpes warm while preparing filling. Reserve 4 anchovy fillets for garnish, and finely chop the remainder. Mix together cheese, anchovies, thick sour cream and lemon juice, then season with salt and pepper, remembering the anchovies are very salty.

Divide filling between crêpes and roll up. Place on a serving dish and sprinkle with chopped parsley. Garnish with reserved anchovy fillets and extra grated cheese and serve at once.

Serves 4.

— SALMON SUPREME CRÊPES —

eight 17.5 cm (7 in) crêpes, see
page 52
1 onion, finely chopped
60 g (2 oz) button mushrooms, thinly
sliced
30 g (1 oz / 6 teaspoons) butter
30 g (1 oz / ¼ cup) plain flour
155 ml (5 fl oz / ⅔ cup) single (light) cream
220 g (7 oz) can red salmon, well drained
and flaked
125 g (4 oz) cooked peas
60 g (2 oz / ½ cup) grated Gruyère cheese
1 teaspoon lemon juice
salt and pepper
30 g (1 oz / ¼ cup) grated Parmesan
cheese
fresh parsley sprig and lemon twist,
to garnish

Keep crêpes warm while preparing
filling. Put onion, mushrooms and
butter into a saucepan and cook
over low heat for 5 minutes, until
onion is soft. Stir in flour and cook
for 1 minute, stirring, then remove
from heat and stir in cream. Cook
over low heat, stirring until thick
and smooth, without boiling.
Remove from heat and stir in
salmon, peas, Gruyère cheese, lemon
juice and salt and pepper.

Preheat oven to 180C (350F/Gas
4). Divide filling between crêpes and
roll up. Put in a single layer in a
shallow ovenproof serving dish,
sprinkle with Parmesan cheese and
warm through in the oven for 25
minutes. Garnish with fresh parsley
sprig and lemon twist and serve at
once.

Serves 4.

— FISH CRESPOLINI —

eight 17.5 cm (7 in) crêpes, see page
52
375 g (12 oz) white fish fillets, such as cod
470 ml (15 fl oz / 2 cups) milk
30 g (1 oz / 6 teaspoons) butter
30 g (1 oz / ¼ cup) plain flour
4 tomatoes, skinned, seeded and chopped
3 teaspoons lemon juice
salt and pepper
90 g (3 oz / ¾ cup) grated Cheddar
cheese
watercress sprigs and sliced cherry
tomatoes, to garnish

Keep crêpes warm while preparing
filling. Put fish into a saucepan with
half the milk and poach until fish is
cooked through but unbroken. Drain
and reserve cooking liquid. Skin and
flake fish and set aside.

Melt butter in a saucepan over
low heat, stir in flour and cook for
30 seconds. Remove from heat and
stir in reserved liquid and remaining
milk. Return to low heat and cook
gently, stirring, until thick and
smooth. Divide sauce in half.

Preheat oven to 190C (375F/Gas
5). Stir fish, tomatoes and lemon
juice into half of the sauce and
season with salt and pepper. Divide
fish mixture between crêpes and
roll up. Put in a single layer in a
shallow ovenproof serving dish. Stir
cheese into remaining sauce and
spoon over crêpes. Heat through
in the oven for 20 minutes, until
sauce is bubbling. Garnish with
watercress sprigs and sliced cherry
tomatoes.

Serves 4.

—— PRAWN & TUNA CRÊPES ——

eight 17.5 cm (7 in) crêpes, see
page 52

45 g (1½ oz/9 teaspoons) butter

1 small green pepper (capsicum), cored,
seeded and finely chopped

15 g (½ oz/6 teaspoons) plain flour

155 ml (5 fl oz/⅔ cup) chicken stock

125 g (4 oz) peeled cooked prawns,
thawed if frozen

220 g (7 oz) can tuna in brine,
drained and flaked

155 ml (5 fl oz/⅔ cup) single (light) cream

salt and pepper

peeled prawns, fresh tarragon sprigs and
lemon slices, to garnish

Keep crêpes warm while preparing
filling. Melt butter in a saucepan,
add green pepper (capsicum) and
cook over low heat until just soft.
Add flour and cook for 1 minute,
stirring well.

Stir in chicken stock and simmer
over low heat, stirring, until thick.
Stir in prawns. Add tuna to pan, stir
in cream and heat through but do
not boil. Season to taste with salt
and pepper.

Preheat oven to 180C (350F/Gas
4). Divide mixture between crêpes.
Roll up and put in a single layer in a
shallow ovenproof serving dish.
Cover with foil and heat in the
oven for 15 minutes. Garnish with
peeled prawns, tarragon sprigs and
lemon slices and serve hot.

Serves 4.

—— CURRIED CHICKEN CRÊPES ——

eight 17.5 cm (7 in) crêpes, see
page 52

1 onion, finely chopped

30 g (1 oz/6 teaspoons) butter

2 teaspoons curry powder

30 g (1 oz/¼ cup) plain flour

315 ml (10 fl oz/1¼ cups) chicken stock

375 g (12 oz) cold cooked chicken,
diced

3 teaspoons lemon juice

salt and pepper

slices of green pepper (capsicum), lemon
and fresh mint sprigs, to garnish

Keep crêpes warm while preparing
filling. Put onion and butter into a
saucepan and cook over low heat
for 5 minutes, until soft. Stir in
curry powder and cook for 30
seconds, then stir in flour and cook
for 30 seconds. Gradually add stock
and bring to the boil, stirring
constantly.

Stir in chicken and lemon juice
and season with salt and pepper.
Stir over low heat for 10 minutes.
Divide chicken mixture between
crêpes, roll up, garnish with slices of
green pepper (capsicum), lemon and
mint sprigs and serve at once.

Serves 4.

BOLOGNESE CRÊPES

eight 17.5 cm (7 in) crêpes, see
page 52
1 small clove garlic, crushed
1 large onion, finely chopped
30 g (1 oz / 6 teaspoons) butter
500 g (1 lb) lean minced beef
30 g (1 oz / ¼ cup) plain flour
440 g (14 oz) can tomatoes
2 teaspoons tomato purée (paste)
salt and pepper
30 g (1 oz / ¼ cup) grated Parmesan cheese
watercress sprigs and tomato halves, to
garnish

Keep crêpes warm while preparing
filling. Put garlic and onion into a
saucepan with butter and cook over
low heat for 5 minutes, until onion
is soft.

Add meat and cook over low heat
for 5 minutes, stirring to break up
meat. Stir in flour and cook for 1
minute, then add tomatoes with
juice and tomato purée (paste). Stir
well and simmer, uncovered, for 10
minutes, until thickened. Season to
taste with salt and pepper.

Put one crêpe on a flameproof
serving plate and spread with some
filling. Top with a second crêpe
and repeat until all the crêpes and
filling are used, finishing with a
crêpe. Sprinkle with Parmesan
cheese, and brown under a hot grill
for 2 minutes. Serve at once, cut
into wedges. Garnish each portion
with watercress sprigs and tomato
halves.

Serves 4.

SWEET & SOUR CRÊPES

eight 17.5 cm (7 in) crêpes, see
page 52
250 g (8 oz) boneless shoulder pork,
cubed
15 g (½ oz / 3 teaspoons) lard
220 g (7 oz) can pineapple pieces in syrup
3 teaspoons redcurrant jelly
3 teaspoons moist brown sugar
3 teaspoons white wine vinegar
3 teaspoons cornflour
155 ml (5 fl oz / ⅔ cup) tomato juice
salt and pepper
fresh watercress sprigs or bean sprouts
and spring onion tassels, to garnish

Keep crêpes warm while preparing
filling. Put pork and lard into a
saucepan and fry over low heat for
10 minutes, until meat is tender and
cooked through.

Drain pineapple, and put syrup
into a pan with redcurrant jelly,
sugar, vinegar, cornflour and tomato
juice, then bring to the boil, stirring
constantly. Simmer, uncovered,
until thick, then stir in pork and
pineapple pieces and season to taste
with salt and pepper.

Preheat oven to 190C (375F/Gas
5). Divide pork mixture between
crêpes. Roll up and put in a single
layer in a shallow ovenproof serving
dish. Cover crêpes with foil and
heat through in the oven for 20
minutes. Garnish with watercress
sprigs or bean sprouts and spring
onion tassels and serve hot, straight
from the dish.

Serves 4.

CARIBBEAN CRÊPES

eight 17.5 cm (7 in) crêpes, see
page 52

4 bananas

2 teaspoons lemon juice

155 ml (5 fl oz / ⅔ cup) whipping cream

30 g (1 oz / 2 tablespoons) dark moist
brown sugar

½ teaspoon grated nutmeg

Keep crêpes warm while preparing
filling. Peel bananas and thinly slice
one, then sprinkle with lemon juice
and set aside. Whip cream to stiff
peaks, and set aside about one-
quarter for decoration.

Mash the remaining bananas and
fold into cream with sugar and
nutmeg. Divide mixture between
crêpes and roll up firmly. Place on a
serving dish and decorate with piped
rosettes of cream and banana
slices sprinkled with nutmeg.

Serves 4.

Variation: To make crêpes into
mini cornets, cut each in half and
roll into cornets. Carefully spoon
the filling into the pockets, then
decorate.

CHERRY & ALMOND LAYER

eight 17.5 cm (7 in) crêpes, see
page 52

440 g (14 oz) can cherries

90 g (3 oz / ¼ cup) cherry jam

3 teaspoons lemon juice

60 g (2 oz / ½ cup) ground almonds

2 ripe eating pears, peeled and
thinly sliced

3 teaspoons icing sugar

Keep crêpes warm while preparing
filling. Drain cherries, reserving
juice. Put jam into a small saucepan
and warm over low heat until just
runny, then stir in 6 teaspoons

cherry juice and the lemon juice,
almonds and pears. Remove from
heat and stir in cherries.

Preheat oven to 160C (325F/Gas
3). Put one crêpe on a large ovenproof serving plate. Spread with
some filling and top with a second
crêpe. Repeat until all the crêpes
and cherry mixture are used, finishing with a crêpe on the top. Heat
through in the oven for 10 minutes,
then sift icing sugar over the top
and serve, cut into wedges.

Serves 4.

— FRENCH CHESTNUT CRÊPES —

eight 17.5 cm (7 in) crêpes, see
page 52

250 g (8 oz) can sweetened chestnut
purée

90 ml (3 fl oz / generous ⅓ cup) orange
juice

3 teaspoons lemon juice

3 teaspoons white rum

30 g (1 oz / 6 teaspoons) butter melted

3 teaspoons icing sugar

Preheat oven to 150C (300F/Gas
2). Spread each crêpe with chestnut

purée and fold into quarters. Place
in a shallow flameproof dish. Mix
together the orange juice, lemon
juice and rum and pour over crêpes.
Cover loosely with foil and heat
through in the oven for 30 minutes.

Remove foil. Brush crêpes with
butter and sprinkle with icing sugar,
then put under a hot grill for 2
minutes, or until glazed. Serve at
once.

Serves 4.

— ORANGE LIQUEUR GÂTEAU —

eight 17.5 cm (7 in) crêpes, see
page 52

250 g (8 oz) can mandarin oranges

2 teaspoons cornflour

3 teaspoons clear honey

3 teaspoons apricot jam

9 teaspoons orange-flavoured liqueur

155 ml (5 fl oz / ⅔ cup) whipping cream

Keep crêpes warm while preparing
filling. Drain oranges well, reserving
the juice, then set aside. Mix cornflour with 3 teaspoons juice and put
remaining juice into a saucepan
with honey and jam. Bring to the
boil and add cornflour mixture,
then stir over low heat until thick
and clear. Stir in 6 teaspoons liqueur.

Put one crêpe on a serving plate.
Arrange a few mandarin oranges on

top and sprinkle with the honey
mixture. Put on a second crêpe and
repeat until all the crêpes, oranges
and liqueur-flavoured mixture are
used, finishing with a crêpe. Arrange
any remaining mandarin oranges on
top.

In a bowl, whip cream to soft
peaks and fold in remaining liqueur.
Put cream in a serving bowl.

Serve the crêpe and orange gâteau
cut into wedges, with the cream
handed separately.

Serves 4.

Variation: Add 2 or 3 sliced kiwi
fruit with the oranges, then pipe
rosettes of cream and decorate with
pieces of fruit.

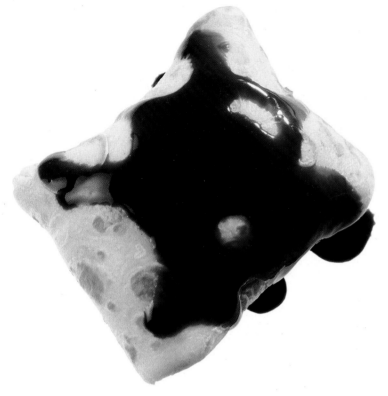

ICE CREAM CRÊPES

eight 17.5 cm (7 in) crêpes, see
page 52
625 ml (20 fl oz) block vanilla ice cream
6 teaspoons cherry brandy
CHOCOLATE SAUCE:
125 g (4 oz / ½ cup) caster sugar
60 g (2 oz / ½ cup) cocoa

To make the chocolate sauce, put
155 ml (5 fl oz/⅔ cup) water and
the sugar into a saucepan and stir
over low heat until sugar has
dissolved. Bring to boil, then simmer for 1 minute. Add cocoa and
return to the boil, beating until
smooth. Set aside and keep warm.

Cut ice cream into 8 cubes and
wrap each one in a crêpe, then put
two crêpes on to each plate. Sprinkle
with cherry brandy and serve at
once with hot chocolate sauce
spooned over.

Serves 4.

APPLE & RUM CRÊPES

eight 17.5 cm (7 in) crêpes, see
page 52
250 g (8 oz) cream cheese
1 eating apple, peeled, cored and sliced
125 g (4 oz / ¾ cup) sultanas
apple slices sprinkled with brown sugar,
to decorate
RUM SAUCE:
60 g (2 oz / ¼ cup) unsalted butter
125 g (4 oz / ¾ cup) moist brown sugar
3 tablespoons whipping cream
60 ml (2 fl oz / ¼ cup) dark rum

To make rum sauce, put butter and
sugar into a bowl, beat until soft and
creamy, then work in the cream and
rum. Turn into a serving bowl and
set aside.

Meanwhile, keep crêpes warm
while preparing filling. Put the
cheese into a bowl and beat until
light and fluffy, then stir in apple
slices and sultanas. Divide mixture
between crêpes and lightly roll up
each. Place in a single layer on a
serving dish and decorate with the
apple slices. Serve with the sauce for
pouring over.

Serves 4.

BASIC OMELETTE

3 eggs
salt and pepper
15 g (½ oz/3 teaspoons) butter
watercress sprig and tomato slice,
to garnish

In a bowl, beat eggs with salt and pepper to taste until just mixed. Put omelette pan over low heat to become thoroughly hot.

Put butter into pan. When butter is sizzling but not brown, pour in eggs. Using a fork or spatula, draw mixture from sides to middle of pan, allowing uncooked egg to run underneath. Repeat 2 or 3 times so egg is pushed up lightly and becomes fluffy. Cook for about 2 minutes, until golden-brown underneath and the top is still slightly runny.

Using a palette knife, fold over one-third of mixture away from handle. Hold over a warm serving plate, with the palm of your hand uppermost. Shake the omelette to the edge of the pan and tip completely over to make another fold. Garnish with watercress and tomato slice and serve at once.

Serves 1.

– SMOKED SALMON OMELETTES –

6 eggs
salt and pepper
30 g (1 oz/6 teaspoons) butter
125 g (4 oz) smoked salmon, finely chopped
1 teaspoon chopped fresh parsley
1 teaspoon chopped fresh chives
fresh chives and smoked salmon, to garnish

In a bowl, beat eggs with salt and pepper to taste. Put omelette pan over low heat to become throughly hot. Melt a little butter in pan, then pour in 6 teaspoons egg and cook until just set. Lift onto a baking sheet and keep warm. Repeat until all the eggs are used.

Mix the smoked salmon with parsley and chives and spoon onto one side of each small omelette. Fold over, garnish with chives and smoked salmon and serve at once.

Serves 4.

—PRAWN SOUFFLÉ OMELETTE—

3 eggs, separated
salt and pepper
30 g (1 oz/6 teaspoons) butter
125 g (4 oz) peeled cooked prawns, thawed if frozen
3 teaspoons lemon juice
1 teaspoon chilli sauce
lemon slice and fresh fennel sprig, to garnish

In a bowl, beat egg yolks with salt and pepper to taste. In a separate bowl, whisk whites to stiff peaks and fold into yolks.

Melt half butter in a 17.5 cm (7 in) omelette pan. Pour in mixture and cook over low heat for 2–3 minutes, until base is set and golden brown.

While omelette is cooking, prepare filling. Put prawns, lemon juice, chilli sauce and remaining butter into a small pan and heat through. Put omelette under high grill for 30 seconds, until lightly browned, then spoon filling over half of the omelette and fold over. Cut in half, garnish with lemon slice and fresh fennel sprig and serve at once.

Serves 2.

– ARNOLD BENNETT OMELETTE –

3 eggs
185 g (6 oz) smoked haddock fillets, cooked, skinned and flaked
salt and pepper
30 g (1 oz/6 teaspoons) butter
75 ml (2½ fl oz/⅓ cup) single (light) cream
60 g (2 oz/½ cup) grated Cheddar cheese
lemon twist and chopped fresh parsley, to garnish

In a bowl, beat eggs lightly, then stir in fish and season to taste with salt and pepper.

Melt butter in a 17.5 cm (7 in) omelette pan. Pour in egg mixture and cook over medium heat, drawing cooked egg from edge of pan towards middle, until just set. Lift onto a warm flameproof serving plate with a palette knife.

Cover omelette with cream and sprinkle with cheese. Put under a medium grill until golden and bubbling. Do not fold, but garnish and serve at once cut in half.

Serves 2.

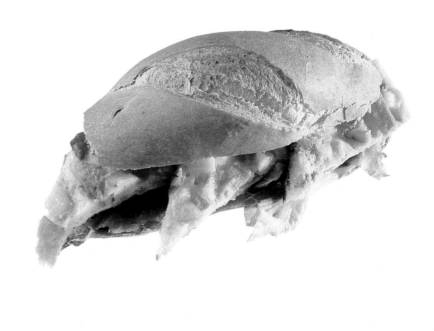

— CHICKEN LIVER OMELETTE —

125 g (4 oz) chicken livers, thawed if frozen and roughly chopped
1 small onion, finely chopped
15 g (½ oz / 3 teaspoons) butter
2 teaspoons chopped fresh thyme
1 teaspoon plain flour
6 teaspoons chicken stock
salt and pepper
one 3-egg Basic Omelette, see page 59
fresh thyme sprigs and grapes, to garnish

Prepare filling before making omelette. Put chicken livers and onion into a small saucepan with butter and cook over low heat for 3 minutes, stirring, until onion is golden. Stir in thyme, flour and stock. Bring to the boil, season to taste with salt and pepper and simmer for 10 minutes.

Make omelette and spoon over chicken liver filling. Fold omelette over. Garnish with thyme sprigs and grapes and serve at once.

Serves 1.

— TORTILLA LOAVES —

4 lean rashers bacon, rinds removed and chopped
15 g (½ oz / 3 teaspoons) butter
250 g (8 oz) cooked potatoes, diced
6 eggs
salt and pepper
4 long bread rolls
butter for spreading
lettuce leaves

Put bacon into a frying pan with butter and fry quickly until fat runs. Stir in potatoes and cook over medium heat until golden.

In a bowl, beat eggs with salt and pepper to taste, then pour over potatoes and cook over medium heat, lifting with a fork, until just set.

Split rolls lengthwise and lightly spread cut sides with butter. Place a lettuce leaf on bottom half of each roll. Cut egg mixture into slices, then place on lettuce and top with upper slices of rolls. Serve hot or cold.

Serves 4.

─── HAM & HERB OMELETTE ───

60 g (2 oz) cooked ham, finely chopped

1 small bunch watercress leaves, finely chopped

15 g (½ oz / 3 teaspoons) butter

salt and pepper

one 3-egg Basic Omelette, see page 59

fresh watercress sprig and ham rolls, to garnish

Prepare filling before making omelette. Put ham and watercress leaves into a small saucepan with butter and shake over low heat for 1 minute to warm through. Remove from heat and season well with salt and pepper.

Make omelette and spoon ham mixture over half of the omelette. Fold over, garnish and serve.

Serves 1.

Note: If fresh watercress isn't available, substitute chopped fresh parsley or chives, or 2 finely chopped spring onions.

─── BREAKFAST OMELETTE ───

2 lean rashers bacon, rinded and finely chopped

15 g (½ oz/3 teaspoons) butter

60 g (2 oz) mushrooms, thinly sliced

3 eggs

salt and pepper

1 tomato, skinned and sliced

fresh mint sprig and halved mushroom, to garnish

Put bacon into a 17.5 cm (7 in) omelette pan with butter and cook over low heat for 2 minutes. Stir in mushrooms and continue cooking over low heat for 2 minutes.

In a bowl, beat eggs with salt and pepper to taste, then pour into pan and top with tomato slices. As eggs cook, draw the mixture from edge of pan to centre so that liquid egg runs to base of pan. When top is just set, slide omelette flat on to serving plate. Garnish with a mint sprig and halved mushroom and serve at once.

Serves 1.

EGG FOO YUNG

4 eggs
3 teaspoons light soy sauce
½ teaspoon salt
3 teaspoons vegetable oil
60 g (2 oz) cooked ham, shredded
90 g (3 oz) bean sprouts
4 spring onions, finely chopped
spring onion brush, to garnish

In a bowl, beat eggs with soy sauce and salt. Heat a 17.5 cm (7 in) omelette pan, add oil, then ham, bean sprouts and onions and cook for 2 minutes, stirring well.

Pour in eggs and stir with a fork until mixture has just set. Put under a hot grill for 1 minute, until golden-brown. Garnish with a spring onion brush and serve at once.

Serves 2.

SPANISH OMELETTE

2 large tomatoes, skinned and chopped
1 small onion, finely chopped
1 small green pepper (capsicum), cored, seeded and finely chopped
1 thick slice cooked ham, diced
1 cooked potato, diced
1 clove garlic, crushed
3 teaspoons olive oil
4 stuffed green olives, sliced
4 eggs
salt and pepper

Put tomatoes, onion, pepper (capsicum), ham, potato and garlic into a large frying pan with oil. Cook over low heat, stirring often, for 7–8 minutes, then stir in olives.

In a bowl, beat eggs with salt and pepper to taste. Pour over vegetables and cook quickly over high heat for 3 minutes. Put under a hot grill for 1 minute until golden. Serve at once.

Serves 2.

—— PIPÉRADE ——

60 g (2 oz/¼ cup) butter
1 large onion, finely sliced
2 green peppers (capsicums), cored, seeded and cut into strips
1 garlic clove, crushed
500 g (1 lb) tomatoes, skinned and finely chopped
salt and pepper
6 eggs
125 g (4 oz) bacon rashers, rinds removed
fresh parsley sprig, to garnish

Melt butter in a large frying pan and cook the onion over low heat for 5 minutes, until softened. Add peppers (capsicums) to the pan with the garlic and gently cook for 5 minutes.

Add tomatoes and salt and pepper to taste and cook, covered, for 20 minutes, stirring occasionally.

In a bowl, beat eggs lightly. Uncover tomato mixture, pour on eggs and cook over low heat, lifting eggs constantly with a fork.

While eggs are cooking, grill bacon rashers until just crisp. Drain well on absorbent kitchen paper. When eggs are just set, lift onto a warm flat serving dish and cover with grilled bacon rashers. Garnish with fresh parsley sprigs and serve at once, cut into quarters.

Serves 4.

—— ITALIAN PIZZA OMELETTE ——

3 teaspoons vegetable oil
1 small onion, finely chopped
220 g (7 oz) can tomatoes
60 g (2 oz) button mushrooms, thinly sliced
pinch of dried marjoram
salt and pepper
two 3-egg Basic Omelettes, see page 59
30 g (1 oz) Mozzarella cheese, thinly sliced
1 tomato, sliced
4 thin slices salami, halved
fresh marjoram sprigs and few capers, to garnish, if desired

Prepare the topping before making the omelettes. Heat the oil in a small saucepan and fry the onion over low heat for 3 minutes, then add tomatoes and their juice, mushrooms, majoram and salt and pepper to taste. Simmer, uncovered, for 10 minutes, until mixture is reduced by half.

Prepare the omelettes and when two-thirds cooked, spoon half the tomato mixture over each one.

Arrange cheese and tomatoes on top, then put under medium grill to set omelettes and melt cheese. Roll salami slices into cones and place 4 on each omelette. Garnish with marjoram and capers, if desired, and serve at once.

Serves 2.

— DIJON SURPRISE OMELETTE —

| 6 eggs |
| 6 teaspoons caster sugar |
| 2 almond macaroon biscuits, crushed |
| 6 teaspoons single (light) cream |
| 30 g (1 oz/6 teaspoons) butter |
| 5 tablespoons blackcurrant jam |
| 30 g (1 oz/¼ cup) finely chopped walnuts |
| TOPPING: |
| 2 egg whites |
| 125 g (4 oz/½ cup) caster sugar |
| 6 teaspoons icing sugar, sifted |

Preheat oven to 220C (425F/Gas 7). In a bowl, beat eggs, sugar, crushed biscuits and cream until thick and creamy. Melt half the butter in a 17.5 cm (7 in) omelette pan, pour in half egg mixture and cook over low heat until just set. Lift on to a warm ovenproof plate, then repeat with remaining egg mixture.

Warm jam in a small saucepan and stir in walnuts. Spread mixture on first omelette and top with other omelette. In a bowl, whisk egg whites to stiff peaks, then fold in caster sugar. Carefully pipe or spread over omelettes, making sure they are completely covered. Sprinkle with icing sugar and bake in the oven for 3 minutes, until meringue is lightly coloured. Serve at once.

Serves 4.

— CHRISTMAS OMELETTE —

| 6 eggs, separated |
| 6 teaspoons caster sugar |
| grated peel of 1 orange |
| 60 ml (2 fl oz/¼ cup) white rum |
| 30 g (1 oz/6 teaspoons) butter |
| 6 tablespoons fruit mincemeat |
| 2 teaspoons icing sugar, sifted |
| holly leaves, to decorate |

In a bowl, beat egg yolks with sugar, orange peel and 3 teaspoons rum. Whisk whites to stiff peaks and fold into yolks.

Melt butter in a 20 cm (8 in) omelette pan, pour in mixture and cook over low heat for 4–5 minutes, until golden-brown underneath.

Warm fruit mincemeat in a saucepan until lukewarm, then spread on half omelette and fold omelette over. Lift onto a warm flameproof serving plate and sprinkle with icing sugar. Place under hot grill for 30 seconds, to melt sugar and glaze.

Put remaining rum into a small saucepan and warm gently, then pour over omelette and ignite at once with a match. Serve as soon as flames die down, decorated with holly leaves.

Serves 3–4.

STUFFED TOMATO SALAD

12 firm tomatoes
90 g (3 oz) curd cheese
1 tablespoon single (light) cream
60 g (2 oz) smoked spiced ham, finely chopped
2.5 cm (1 in) piece cucumber, peeled and finely chopped
2 teaspoons chopped fresh dill or chives
a few salad leaves, to serve
1-2 tablespoons vinaigrette
cucumber slices, to garnish

Cut tops off tomatoes with a serrated-edge knife. With the tip of the knife, cut round insides and scoop out seeds with a small spoon. Turn tomato shells upside-down on absorbent kitchen paper to drain.

Put cheese and cream into a bowl and beat until smooth. Stir in chopped ham, cucumber and chopped dill or chives. Spoon into tomatoes shells, then replace lids. In a bowl, toss salad leaves in dressing until well coated, then arrange on 4 plates. Place 3 tomatoes on each plate, and serve garnished with slices of cucumber.

Serves 4.

Variations: Use larger tomatoes and cut in half to give a vandyked edge, or cut the tomatoes into basket shapes.

CELERIAC & MUSSELS

750 g (1 ½ lb) celeriac
2 tablespoons lemon juice
1 kg (2 lb) fresh mussels, scrubbed and debearded
2 tablespoons dry white wine
RÉMOULADE SAUCE:
75 ml (2½ fl oz/⅓ cup) mayonnaise
2 teaspoons chopped gherkins
1 teaspoon chopped capers
1 teaspoon chopped fresh parsley
1 teaspoon anchovy paste

Peel celeriac and cut into thin slices. Immediately put into a saucepan half-full of boiling water with lemon juice. Simmer for 4-5 minutes or until just tender. Drain, then cut into thin strips and put into a bowl to cool.

Put mussels into a large saucepan with wine, cover and cook over a high heat for about 5 minutes until mussels open. Remove from heat and discard any which remain closed. Strain mussels, reserving broth. Reserve a few mussels in the shells for garnish. Remove remainder from shells and add to celeriac.

To make sauce, put ingredients into a bowl with 2-3 tablespoons of reserved broth, then mix together to give a consistency of thick cream. Stir into celeriac and mussels.

Spoon into a serving dish or 4 individual dishes and garnish with reserved mussels.

Serves 4.

KIPPER SALAD

3 large natural smoked kippers
2 tablespoons virgin olive oil
60 ml (2 fl oz/¼ cup) lemon juice
1 teaspoon sugar
1 onion, sliced
1 bay leaf
lemon slices and mustard and cress, to garnish

Bone and skin kippers. Slice fillets and put into a glass dish. Pour over the oil and lemon juice. Add the sugar, onion and bay leaf, then mix together. Cover the dish and refrigerate for about 24 hours.

Drain kipper pieces and onion and divide between 4 plates. Serve garnished with lemon slices and mustard and cress.

Serves 4.

INDONESIAN SEAFOOD SALAD

375 g (12 oz) unpeeled cooked prawns
1 tablespoon sunflower oil
1 small onion, finely chopped
1 clove garlic, crushed
3 tomatoes, skinned, seeded and chopped
3 teaspoons dark soy sauce
1 teaspoon ground ginger
1 green chilli, seeded and finely chopped
1 tablespoon red wine vinegar
250 g (8 oz) prepared squid
red or green pepper (capsicum) strips, to garnish

Peel the prawns, leaving the tail shells intact but discarding the rest of the shells. Set aside prawns.

Heat the oil in a saucepan and cook the onion until soft. Add garlic, tomatoes, soy sauce, ginger, chilli and vinegar and simmer for 5 minutes.

Stir rings of squid, tentacles and prawns into sauce and cook, uncovered, for 5 minutes. Allow seafood to cool in sauce. To serve, divide seafood and sauce between 4 dishes and garnish with strips of pepper (capsicum).

Serves 4.

— AVOCADO CRAB LOUIS —

2 avocados
1 tablespoon lemon juice
250 g (8 oz) white crabmeat, well drained if canned and flaked
fresh chervil sprigs, to garnish
brown bread and butter, to serve
SEAFOOD SAUCE:
60 ml (2 fl oz/¼ cup) mayonnaise
1 tablespoon tomato ketchup (sauce)
½ teaspoon Worcestershire sauce
60 ml (2 fl oz/¼ cup) single (light) cream
2 teaspoons lemon juice
1 teaspoon dry sherry
pinch cayenne pepper

Halve the avocados, remove the stones, then peel. Slice and brush with lemon juice to prevent discoloration. Then arrange the slices on 4 plates.

To make sauce, mix ingredients together in a bowl, then fold in crabmeat.

Divide the crabmeat mixture between the plates, then garnish each with sprigs of fresh chervil. Serve the salads with brown bread and butter.

Serves 4.

— LAMB & NOODLE SQUASH —

1 boneless, rolled saddle joint of lamb, weighing about 750 g (1½ lb)
1 clove garlic, slivered
salt and pepper
rosemary sprigs
1 noodle (spaghetti) squash, weighing about 750 g (1½ lb)
cooked frozen peas and rosemary sprigs, to garnish
RED PEPPER DRESSING:
1 small red pepper (capsicum), roasted and skinned
1 teaspoon sherry vinegar
3 tablespoons virgin olive oil

Preheat oven to 200C (400F/Gas 6). With a sharp knife, make incisions in the lamb and push in slivers of garlic. Season lamb with salt and pepper, then place in a roasting tin with sprigs of rosemary. Cook in the oven for 40 minutes.

Meanwhile, cut the squash in half, discard the seeds, then place in a roasting pan, cut side down, with enough water to come halfway up sides of pan. Simmer for 15-20 minutes until squash is tender. Remove from the pan and scoop out the centre into a colander. Drain.

To make the dressing, remove core and seeds from the pepper and put the flesh into a blender or food processor with the vinegar and oil, work until smooth. Season with salt and pepper and set aside.

Remove lamb from oven and stand for 5 minutes. Divide squash between 6 plates. Slice lamb and arrange on the plates. Spoon over dressing and garnish with a few peas and sprigs of rosemary.

Serves 6 as a main course.

— ORIENTAL CHICKEN SALAD —

2 cooked chicken breasts (fillets), skinned
185 g (6 oz) beansprouts, trimmed
125 g (4 oz) button mushrooms, sliced
1 yellow pepper (capsicum), seeded and diced
3 spring onions, chopped
2 carrots, cut into matchsticks
½ quantity salad dressing
toasted sesame seeds and radish flowers, to garnish

Shred chicken and put into a bowl with beansprouts, mushrooms, pepper (capsicum), spring onions, and carrots; mix together.

Pour the dressing over the salad, toss together, then transfer to a serving dish. Sprinkle over the sesame seeds and garnish with radish flowers. Serve at once.

Serves 4.

— CORONATION CHICKEN —

2 kg (4 lb) chicken, cooked
paprika
1 carrot, sliced and cut into flowers and 1 stick celery, cut into thin strips, to garnish
CURRY MAYONNAISE:
60 ml (2 fl oz/½ cup) mayonnaise
2 tablespoons lemon juice
2 tablespoons single (light) cream
5 tablespoons natural yogurt
1 teaspoon tomato purée (paste)
1 teaspoon curry paste
2 tablespoons mango chutney

Remove the chicken meat from bones, discarding skin and bones. Divide meat into neat pieces and place on a serving platter.

To make the Curry Mayonnaise, put all the ingredients into a blender or food processor and work until smooth. Pour over the chicken and dust with paprika. Serve garnished with carrot flowers and celery.

Serves 6.

PINK TROUT SALAD

2 large pink trout, cleaned
salt and pepper
a little oil
4 carrots
2 courgettes (zucchini)
15 cm (6 in) piece cucumber
½ carton alfalfa sprouts
1 Webb's lettuce, separated into leaves
tarragon sprigs and nasturtium flowers, to garnish
TARRAGON VINAIGRETTE:
½ quantity vinaigrette dressing
3 teaspoons freshly chopped tarragon

Season trout with salt and pepper and brush with a little oil. Cook under a preheated grill for 10-15 minutes, until fish flakes when tested, turning once. Allow to cool.

Using a potato peeler, pare thin slices off the carrots, discarding centres, and put into a bowl.

Cut courgettes diagonally to give large, thin slices. Blanch in a saucepan of boiling water for 1 minute. Drain, rinse under cold water and drain again. Add to the carrots.

Using a canelle knife, cut strips of peel from cucumber and discard. Cut the cucumber in half lengthwise, then slice across. Add to the bowl with the alfalfa sprouts.

To make the dressing, mix ingredients together in a bowl or screwtop jar. Pour over salad, toss gently, divide between 4 plates. Arrange lettuce leaves on the plates. Skin and bone trout. Cut flesh into neat pieces and arrange on the salad. Serve garnished with sprigs of tarragon and nasturtium flowers.

Serves 4.

GERMAN SAUSAGE SALAD

two 200 g (7 oz) small sticks German sausage, such as salami, bierwurst or Bavarian ham sausage
½ Webb's or iceberg lettuce, shredded
1 red pepper (capsicum), seeded and diced
1 green pepper (capsicum), seeded and diced
1 large head chicory, thinly sliced
½ cucumber, diced
1 quantity vinaigrette dressing
1 teaspoon poppy seeds, to garnish

Remove skins from the sausages and dice. Put lettuce into a glass serving bowl, scatter over half the diced sausage. Add a layer of peppers, then remaining diced sausage. Add chicory and cucumber, then pour over dressing.

Serve sprinkled with poppy seeds.

Serves 4-6.

FONDUE BOURGUIGNONNE

BACON PARCELS

1 kg (2 lb) fillet steak

TOMATO SAUCE: 1 tablespoon oil
2 shallots, finely chopped
1 clove garlic, crushed
440 g (14 oz) can chopped tomatoes
2 tablespoons tomato purée (paste)
salt and pepper
1 tablespoon chopped fresh parsley

To make tomato sauce, heat oil in a saucepan, add shallots and cook gently until soft.

Stir in garlic, tomatoes with their juice and tomato purée (paste). Season with salt and pepper, bring to the boil, then reduce heat and simmer, uncovered, for about 30 minutes or until sauce has reduced and thickened. Stir in parsley and serve hot or cold.

Cut the steak into 2.5 cm (1 in) cubes and put into a serving dish. Each person spears a cube of meat with a fondue fork and immerses the meat in the hot oil to fry. The meat cube is cooked according to individual taste.

Serves 4-6.

375 g (12 oz) streaky bacon, rinds removed
250 g (8 oz) chicken livers

DEVILLED SAUCE: 15 g (½ oz) butter
1 shallot, finely chopped
3 teaspoons plain flour
155 ml (5 fl oz/⅔ cup) chicken stock
4 tomatoes, skinned and chopped
1 tablespoon tomato purée (paste)
2 teaspoons sugar
1 tablespoon red wine vinegar
3 teaspoons Worcestershire sauce
½ teaspoon paprika
pinch of cayenne pepper

Cut rashers in half; cut livers into pieces.

Wrap bacon around chicken livers and spear onto bamboo skewers Place on a serving plate.

To make devilled sauce, melt butter in a saucepan, add shallot and cook until soft. Stir in flour, then add stock and remaining ingredients. Simmer for 15 minutes, then strain sauce and serve hot with the bacon parcels cooked in the hot oil.

Serves 4.

VEAL MILANESE

750 g (1½ lb) leg veal, cubed
3 tablespoons seasoned plain flour
3 eggs, beaten
125 g (4 oz/1 cup) dry breadcrumbs
2 teaspoons finely grated lemon peel

ITALIAN SAUCE: 2 tablespoons olive oil
1 onion, finely chopped
1-2 cloves garlic, crushed
750 g (1½ lb) ripe tomatoes, skinned and chopped
5 tablespoons dry white wine
salt and pepper
1 tablespoon chopped fresh basil

Toss veal in flour; dip in egg and coat in mixed crumbs and peel.

To make Italian sauce, heat oil in a saucepan, add onion and garlic and cook over a low heat until soft. Add tomatoes and wine and season with salt and pepper. Simmer for 30 minutes.

Purée sauce in a blender or food processor until smooth, or press through a sieve. Stir in basil and reheat sauce before serving. Serve with the veal cooked in hot oil.

Serves 4-6.

SPICY CHICKEN FONDUE

6 boned and skinned chicken breasts
4 tablespoons oil
2 teaspoons paprika
½ teaspoon chilli powder

CURRY SAUCE: 1 tablespoon oil
1 onion, finely chopped
2 teaspoons mild curry powder
3 teaspoons plain flour
315 ml (10 fl oz/1¼ cups) milk
6 teaspoons mango chutney
salt and pepper

Cut chicken into 2 cm (¾ in) pieces and mix with oil, paprika and chilli powder.

Place chicken on a serving plate. To make curry sauce, heat oil in a saucepan, add onion and cook until soft. Stir in curry powder and cook for 2 minutes, then stir in flour.

Gradually stir in milk and bring slowly to the boil, stirring all the time. Continue to cook until sauce thickens. Simmer for 5 minutes, then add chutney and season with salt and pepper. Serve hot with the chicken cooked in the hot oil.

Serves 4-6.

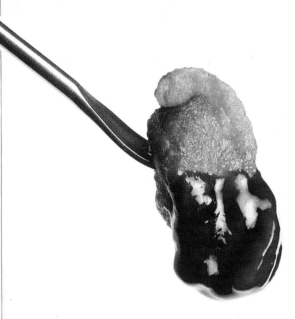

FRUITY DUCK FONDUE

750 g (1½ lb) duck breast fillets, cut in pieces
6 teaspoons seasoned flour
1 teaspoon five-spice powder

MARMALADE SAUCE: 1 tablespoon demerara sugar
155 ml (5 fl oz/⅔ cup) orange juice
4 tablespoons mature orange marmalade
juice of 1 lemon
60 g (2 oz/⅓ cup) raisins, chopped if large

WINE AND CHERRY SAUCE: 1 tablespoon sugar
375 g (12 oz) can black cherries, drained
90 ml (3 fl oz/⅓ cup) red wine
pinch of mixed spice

Toss duck in flour and five-spice powder.

Place duck on a serving plate. To make marmalade sauce, put all the ingredients into a small saucepan and simmer for 5 minutes.

To make wine and cherry sauce. Put all ingredients into a saucepan and simmer for 15 minutes. Press through a sieve, discarding the stones. Serve sauces warm with the duck cooked in the hot oil.

Serves 4.

CHEESY MEATBALL FONDUE

750 g (1½ lb) lean minced beef
1 tablespoon finely chopped onion
30 g (1 oz/½ cup) fresh wholemeal breadcrumbs
salt and pepper
125 g (4 oz) Cheddar cheese, diced

TANGY SAUCE: 1 tablespoon tomato purée (paste)
1 tablespoon red wine vinegar
2 tablespoons honey
2 teaspoons dry mustard
1 tablespoon Worcestershire sauce
315 ml (10 fl oz/1¼ cups) chicken stock
2 teaspoons cornflour
juice of 1 orange

Mix together beef, onion and breadcrumbs.

Season meat mixture with salt and pepper and divide into 30 balls. Flatten each ball out, place a piece of cheese in centre, then mould meat around cheese, sealing it well to enclose cheese completely.

To make tangy sauce, put tomato purée (paste), wine vinegar, honey, mustard, Worcestershire sauce and stock into a saucepan and simmer for 10 minutes. Blend cornflour smoothly with orange juice, then stir into the sauce and simmer for 1 minute, stirring all the time. Serve with the meatballs cooked in the hot oil.

Serves 6.

Note: Serve also with Relish Sauce, see page 74.

MINCED LAMB FONDUE

625 g (1¼ lb) minced lean lamb
3 spring onions, finely chopped
60 g (2 oz/1 cup) fresh breadcrumbs
2 tablespoons chopped fresh parsley
salt and pepper

MUSHROOM SAUCE: 60 g (2 oz/¼ cup) butter
185 g (6 oz) mushrooms, finely chopped
6 teaspoons plain flour
315 ml (10 fl oz/1¼ cups) milk
1 tablespoon dry sherry

Put all the ingredients for the lamb balls into a bowl. Season with salt and pepper and mix together.

With wetted hands, shape mixture into 20-24 balls, the size of a walnut, and place on a serving plate.

To make mushroom sauce, melt butter in a saucepan, add mushrooms and cook gently for 5 minutes. Stir in flour, then slowly add milk and bring to the boil, stirring. Simmer for a further 5 minutes, then season with salt and pepper and add sherry. Serve warm with the lamb balls cooked in the hot oil.

Serves 4-6.

Note: Serve also with Devilled Sauce, see page 71.

CRISPY SAUSAGE BITES

500 g (1 lb) pork sausagemeat
1 small onion, finely chopped
90 g (3 oz/⅓ cup) cream cheese
1 tablespoon chopped fresh parsley
1 teaspoon prepared mustard
30 g (1 oz/½ cup) fresh breadcrumbs
salt and pepper
2 eggs, beaten
90 g (3 oz/¾ cup) dry breadcrumbs

RELISH SAUCE: Tomato Sauce, see page 71
2 tablespoons sweet pickle relish

Put sausagemeat and onion into a frying pan; cook until lightly brown and crumbly.

Turn into a bowl and add cream cheese, parsley, mustard, fresh breadcrumbs and season with salt and pepper. Shape into 16-20 small firm balls, moulding to make them smooth. Dip first in beaten egg, then roll in dry breadcrumbs until evenly coated. Chill until required.

To make relish sauce, put tomato sauce in a saucepan, stir in relish and heat through. Serve warm. Each person spears a sausage ball with a fondue fork and immerses it in the hot oil to fry until crisp and golden.

Serves 4.

MIDDLE EASTERN FONDUE

750 g (1½ lb) lean leg of lamb, cubed

MARINADE: 3 tablespoons olive oil
1 tablespoon lemon juice
1 clove garlic, crushed
1 tablespoon chopped fresh mint
1 teaspoon ground cinnamon
salt and pepper

APRICOT SAUCE: 1 tablespoon oil
1 shallot, finely chopped
440 g (14 oz) can apricots in natural juice
1 tablespoon chopped fresh parsley

Mix marinade ingredients together and pour over cubed lamb.

Cover lamb mixture and leave to marinate for at least 2 hours, or preferably overnight. To make apricot sauce, heat oil in a saucepan, add shallot and cook over a low heat until soft. Add apricots and the juice and simmer for 5 minutes.

Purée sauce in a blender or food processor, then season with salt and pepper and stir in parsley. Reheat before serving. Remove lamb from marinade and arrange on a serving plate when ready to serve and cook in the hot oil.

Serves 4.

Note: Serve also with Cucumber Yogurt Sauce, see page 77.

MEXICAN FONDUE

1 kg (2 lb) lean rump steak

MEXICAN SAUCE: 1 tablespoon oil
½ a Spanish onion, finely chopped
1 clove garlic, crushed
440 g (14 oz) can tomatoes
2 tablespoons tomato purée (paste)
½ teaspoon chilli powder
1 fresh green chilli, seeded and finely chopped
salt and pepper

Cut meat into 2.5 cm (1 in) cubes and put onto a serving plate.

To make Mexican sauce, heat oil in a saucepan, add onion and garlic and cook gently until softened. Stir in tomatoes and their juice, tomato purée (paste) and chilli powder. Simmer, uncovered, for 10 minutes.

Remove sauce from heat and purée in a blender or food processor until smooth, or press through a sieve to give a smooth sauce. Return to the heat, add chopped chilli and simmer for a further 15 minutes. Season with salt and pepper. Serve with the meat cooked in the hot oil.

Serves 4-6.

Note: Serve also with Cool Avocado Dip, see page 77.

PORK SATAY

½ teaspoon chilli powder
1 teaspoon ground coriander
½ teaspoon turmeric
3 teaspoons oil
3 teaspoons soy sauce
½ teaspoon salt
1 kg (2 lb) pork fillet, cubed

PEANUT SAUCE: 60 g (2 oz/⅔ cup) desiccated coconut
315 ml (10 fl oz/1¼ cups) boiling water
5 tablespoons crunchy peanut butter
2 teaspoons sugar
1 fresh green chilli, seeded and finely chopped
1 teaspoon lemon juice
1 clove garlic, crushed

In a bowl, mix together spices, oil, soy sauce and salt to make a paste. Add pork and with wet hands, knead paste into meat. Cover bowl and leave in the refrigerator for at least 2 hours.

To make peanut sauce, put coconut into a bowl, pour over boiling water and leave to stand for 15 minutes. Strain mixture into a saucepan, pressing well to extract all moisture. Discard coconut. Add remaining ingredients and mix well. Cook over a low heat, stirring until the sauce comes to the boil. Serve hot with the meat cooked in hot oil.

Serves 4-6.

TERIYAKI FONDUE

1 kg (2 lb) fillet steak
3 teaspoons light soft brown sugar
125 ml (4 fl oz/½ cup) soy sauce
6 tablespoons dry sherry
2 cloves garlic, crushed
1 teaspoon ground ginger

BEANSPROUT SALAD: 1 small head Chinese leaves
250 g (8 oz) fresh beansprouts
1 red pepper (capsicum), seeded and finely sliced
½ bunch spring onions, shredded
6 tablespoons sunflower oil
1 tablespoon wine vinegar

Cut steak into thin strips 1 cm (½ in) wide and 10 cm (4 in) long.

Put 1 teaspoon of sugar and 2 tablespoons of soy sauce into a bowl and set aside. In a large bowl, combine remaining sugar and soy sauce, sherry, garlic and ginger. Add strips of meat and leave to marinate for 1 hour. Weave the strips of meat onto 20-24 bamboo skewers ready for cooking in hot oil.

To prepare the salad, shred Chinese leaves and put into a bowl with beansprouts, pepper (capsicum) and spring onions. Add oil to reserved sugar and soy sauce, then whisk in vinegar and pour over salad. Toss lightly together.

Serves 4-6.

ACCOMPANIMENTS

COOL AVOCADO DIP

1 ripe avocado
2 teaspoons lemon juice
155 ml (5 fl oz/²⁄₃ cup) thick sour cream
1 teaspoon grated onion
salt and pepper
slice of lemon, to garnish

Cut avocado in half, discard stone, then scoop out flesh into a bowl. Mash flesh with lemon juice until smooth. Stir in sour cream, grated onion and season with salt and pepper. Serve chilled, garnished with a slice of lemon.

ANCHOVY MAYONNAISE

45 g (1½ oz) can anchovies
6 tablespoons mayonnaise
2 tablespoons single (light) cream
2 tablespoons olive oil
1 teaspoon tomato purée (paste)
chopped fresh parsley, to garnish

Drain anchovies and put into a blender with remaining ingredients. Blend ingredients until smooth. Serve chilled, garnished with chopped parsley.

HORSERADISH SAUCE

155 ml (5 fl oz/²⁄₃ cup) double (thick) cream
1 tablespoon grated horseradish
2 spring onions, chopped
salt and pepper
chopped fresh chives, to garnish

In a bowl, whip cream until softly peaking, then stir in remaining ingredients and season with salt and pepper. Serve chilled, garnished with chopped chives.

ACCOMPANIMENTS

CUCUMBER YOGURT SAUCE

125 g (4 oz) low fat soft cheese
155 ml (5 fl oz/²⁄₃ cup) natural yogurt
½ a cucumber, peeled and finely diced
2 teaspoons lemon juice
salt and pepper
chopped cucumber, to garnish

In a bowl, beat cheese and yogurt together until smooth. Add cucumber, lemon juice and season with salt and pepper. Serve chilled, garnished with chopped cucumber.

SPICY ORIENTAL SAUCE

2 tablespoons soy sauce
juice of ½ a lemon
2 fresh green chillies, seeded and chopped
1 clove garlic, crushed
2 teaspoons sesame oil

Put all the ingredients into a bowl and mix together. Serve chilled.

MUSTARD SAUCE

3 teaspoons Dijon mustard
155 ml (5 fl oz/²⁄₃ cup) thick sour cream
3 tablespoons mayonnaise
salt and pepper
crushed mustard seeds or wholegrain mustard,
   to garnish

Put all the ingredients into a bowl and mix well together until smooth. Season with salt and pepper. Serve chilled, garnished with mustard seeds or wholegrain mustard.

COEURS À LA CRÈME

250 g (8 oz) ricotta or cottage cheese
30 g (1 oz/5 teaspoons) caster sugar
1 teaspoon lemon juice
315 ml (10 fl oz/1¼ cups) double (thick) cream
2 egg whites

TO SERVE: **fresh fruit**
double (thick) cream

Line 8 heart-shaped moulds with muslin.
Press cheese through a sieve into a bowl. Stir
in sugar and lemon juice.

In a separate bowl, whip cream until stiff. Stir
into cheese mixture. Whisk egg whites until
stiff, then fold into the cheese mixture.

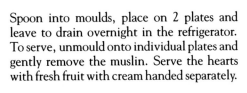

Spoon into moulds, place on 2 plates and
leave to drain overnight in the refrigerator.
To serve, unmould onto individual plates and
gently remove the muslin. Serve the hearts
with fresh fruit with cream handed separately.

Serves 8.

Note: To add extra colour, decorate with
sprigs of redcurrants and blackcurrants.

ORANGE CARAMEL CREAM

125 g (4 oz/½ cup) granulated sugar
3 eggs
8 teaspoons caster sugar
315 ml (10 fl oz/1¼ cups) milk
3 teaspoons sweet orange oil
1 orange
fresh herbs, to decorate

Preheat oven to 180C (350F/Gas 4). Warm 4
china ramekin dishes or 4 dariole moulds. Put
granulated sugar and 3 tablespoons water into
a small saucepan and place over a low heat to
dissolve sugar. Increase heat and boil steadily,
without stirring, to a rich brown caramel.

Divide between the dishes or moulds, tipping
them to cover bottom and sides with caramel.
Set aside. In a bowl, beat eggs and caster sugar
together. Heat milk until almost boiling,
then pour over egg mixture, beating all the
time. Stir in orange oil.

Strain mixture into dishes or moulds. Grate
orange peel finely, divide between dishes and
stir in. Place dishes in a roasting tin, pour in
boiling water to come halfway up the sides,
then bake in the oven for about 20 minutes,
until set. Cool in the dishes, then chill until
required. Turn out onto serving plates, and
decorate with segments cut from the grated
orange and herb leaves.

Serves 4.

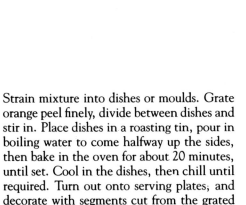

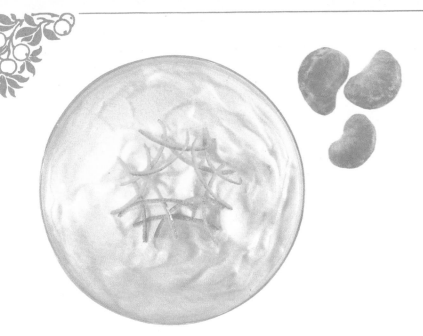

TANGERINE SYLLABUB

BANANA BRÛLÉE

grated peel and juice of 3 tangerines
grated peel and juice of 1 lemon
90 g (3 oz/⅓ cup) caster sugar
90 ml (3 fl oz/⅓ cup) cream sherry
315 ml (10 fl oz/1¼ cups) double (thick) cream
extra grated peel, to decorate, if desired

625 ml (20 fl oz/2½ cups) whipping cream
3 large bananas
juice of 1 small lemon
60 g (2 oz/¼ cup) caster sugar
few crumbled meringues, if desired
125 g (4 oz/½ cup) granulated sugar

Put tangerine and lemon peel and both juices into a bowl with sugar and sherry and leave to infuse in a cool place for at least 1 hour.

In a large bowl, whip cream until thick. Slice bananas thinly into a separate bowl and toss in lemon juice.

In a large bowl, whip the cream while gradually pouring in the infused mixture. Keep whipping until mixture is thick enough to form soft peaks.

Fold bananas and caster sugar into whipped cream with crumbled meringues, if using. Spoon the mixture into a serving dish and place in the refrigerator.

Pour mixture into a glass serving bowl or individual glasses and chill for at least 2 hours before serving. Decorate with extra peel, if desired.

Serves 4-6.

Note: Use a sharp grater to grate the peel of tangerines, otherwise the peel tends to tear. Warm citrus fruits slightly before squeezing and they will yield more juice.

Put granulated sugar and 1 tablespoon water into a small saucepan and place over a low heat to dissolve sugar. Do not stir. When sugar has dissolved, increase heat and boil syrup to a rich brown caramel. Immediately dribble this over banana cream mixture, then replace in refrigerator for caramel to harden. Serve within 1-2 hours.

Serves 6.

COFFEE BOMBE

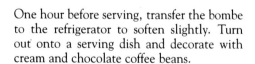

3 eggs, separated
185 g (6 oz/¾ cup) caster sugar
75 ml (2½ fl oz/⅓ cup) cold strong black coffee
500 ml (16 fl oz/2 cups) double (thick) cream
155 g (5 oz) meringues
whipped cream and chocolate coffee beans, to decorate

In a large bowl, beat egg yolks and sugar together until thick and mousse-like. Gently stir in coffee. In a separate bowl, whip cream lightly. Crush meringues.

Fold cream and meringues into coffee mixture. In a large bowl, whisk egg whites until stiff and fold 1 tablespoon into coffee mixture. Tip egg whites onto coffee mixture, then fold together carefully. Pour into a 2 litre (64 fl oz/8 cup) lightly oiled bombe mould and freeze until firm.

One hour before serving, transfer the bombe to the refrigerator to soften slightly. Turn out onto a serving dish and decorate with cream and chocolate coffee beans.

Serves 8.

Note: To turn out bombe, wring out a tea-towel in very hot water and wrap it around the mould. Invert onto a serving plate and lift off mould.

CHARLOTTE RUSSE

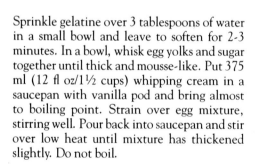

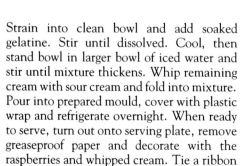

16 sponge fingers
3 teaspoons powdered gelatine
4 egg yolks
90 g (3 oz/⅓ cup) caster sugar
625 ml (20 fl oz/2½ cups) whipping cream
1 vanilla pod, split open
315 ml (10 fl oz/1¼ cups) thick sour cream
185 g (6 oz) fresh raspberries
whipped cream, to decorate

Line the base of 1.1 litre (35 fl oz/4¼ cup) charlotte mould with greaseproof paper. Stand sponge fingers, pressing against each other, round sides of mould and trim to fit.

Sprinkle gelatine over 3 tablespoons of water in a small bowl and leave to soften for 2-3 minutes. In a bowl, whisk egg yolks and sugar together until thick and mousse-like. Put 375 ml (12 fl oz/1½ cups) whipping cream in a saucepan with vanilla pod and bring almost to boiling point. Strain over egg mixture, stirring well. Pour back into saucepan and stir over low heat until mixture has thickened slightly. Do not boil.

Strain into clean bowl and add soaked gelatine. Stir until dissolved. Cool, then stand bowl in larger bowl of iced water and stir until mixture thickens. Whip remaining cream with sour cream and fold into mixture. Pour into prepared mould, cover with plastic wrap and refrigerate overnight. When ready to serve, turn out onto serving plate, remove greaseproof paper and decorate with the raspberries and whipped cream. Tie a ribbon round pudding.

Serves 6-8.

OEUFS À LA NEIGE

RED BERRY SOUFFLÉ

4 eggs, separated
scant ½ teaspoon cornflour
90 g (3 oz/⅓ cup) caster sugar
125 ml (4 fl oz/½ cup) milk
315 ml (10 fl oz/1¼ cups) single (light) cream
1 vanilla pod
1 tablespoon orange flower water
1 tablespoon toasted, flaked almonds
orange peel strips, to decorate

In a bowl, cream egg yolks with cornflour and one-third of the caster sugar. Place milk, cream and vanilla pod in a saucepan and scald (bring to near boiling point).

30 g (1 oz/6 teaspoons) butter
125 g (4 oz/½ cup) caster sugar, plus 1 extra tablespoon
250 g (8 oz) mixed soft red fruits, fresh or frozen, thawed if frozen
1 tablespoon Fraise liqueur or crème de cassis
5 egg whites
icing sugar, to serve

Preheat oven to 180C (350F/Gas 4). Use the butter to grease a 1 litre (32 fl oz/4 cup) soufflé dish or 6 individual dishes, then dust out with 1 tablespoon caster sugar.

Pour the hot milk over the egg yolks, whisking all the time. Place bowl over a saucepan of simmering water and cook gently, stirring, until it is the consistency of double cream. Cool, remove vanilla pod and stir in orange flower water. In a large bowl, whisk egg whites until stiff, add remaining sugar and whisk again.

Purée fruit, liqueur and remaining caster sugar together in a blender or food processor. Turn into a bowl. In a separate bowl, whisk egg whites until stiff, but not dry. Fold 1 tablespoon into fruit purée, then tip purée onto whites and fold together carefully, using a metal spoon.

Fill a large saucepan with water and bring to simmering point. Put spoonfuls of meringue mixture, a few at a time, into water and poach for 5 minutes, turning carefully once. (There should be enough meringue for 4 spoonfuls per portion.) Drain on absorbent kitchen paper and cool. Pour most of the custard into a glass serving bowl and arrange meringue puffs on top. Drizzle the remaining custard over meringues, then sprinkle with flaked almonds. Decorate with orange peel.

Serves 4.

Spoon mixture into prepared soufflé dish, place on a baking sheet and bake in the oven for 25-30 minutes for the large soufflé; 15-20 minutes for the individual soufflés, until risen and just set. Dust with a little icing sugar and serve immediately.

Serves 6.

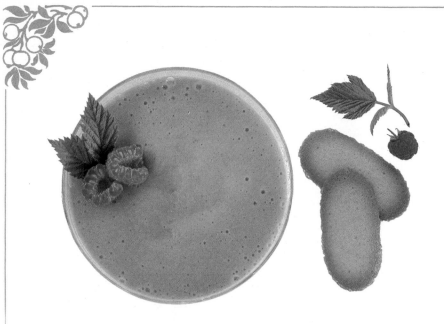

FRAMBOISE ZABAGLIONE

4 egg yolks
220 ml (7 fl oz/⁷⁄₈ cup) Framboise liqueur
30 g (1 oz/5 teaspoons) caster sugar
strawberries or raspberries, to decorate, if desired
langues de chat biscuits, to serve

Put egg yolks, liqueur and sugar into a double boiler or a bowl set over a saucepan of simmering water.

Set over a medium heat and, using a balloon whisk, whisk the mixture until it is very thick and mousse-like in appearance – this will take about 20 minutes.

Pour mixture into glasses, decorate with strawberries or raspberries if desired, and serve immediately, while still warm, with langues de chat biscuits.

Serves 4.

Note: Although it is laborious it is important to use a hand whisk for this recipe. An electric whisk increases the volume of the eggs too quickly, so that they do not have a chance to cook. The mixture will then collapse when it is poured into glasses.

CHOCOLATE TRIFLE

100 g (3½ oz) plain (dark) chocolate
4 tablespoons rum and water, mixed
4 egg yolks
1 tablespoon caster sugar
750 ml (24 fl oz/3 cups) whipping cream
250 g (8 oz) plain or trifle sponge cakes
185 g (6 oz/½ cup) apricot jam
375 g (12 oz) mixed fruit, such as grapes, ripe pears and bananas
grated chocolate, to decorate

Melt chocolate with rum and water in a double boiler or a bowl set over a saucepan of simmering water. Set over medium heat and stir until smooth.

In a large bowl, whisk egg yolks and sugar together until light and fluffy. Put 315 ml (10 fl oz/1¼ cups) cream into a pan and bring almost to boiling point. Whisk into yolk mixture with chocolate. Return mixture to saucepan and whisk over a very low heat until chocolate is incorporated and mixture has thickened slightly. Slice sponges in half. Warm jam slightly in a small saucepan, then brush over the sponges.

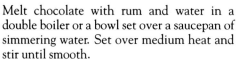

Place sponges in a glass serving bowl or individual glass dishes. To prepare fruit, halve and seed grapes, peel, core and finely slice pears and slice bananas. Scatter fruit over sponges. Lightly whip remaining cream, then spoon chocolate sauce over fruit and spread half the cream over it. Continue whisking remaining cream to stiff peaks and use to decorate, then sprinkle with grated chocolate. Chill in the refrigerator until ready to serve.

Serves 6.

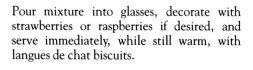

MIXED CHOCOLATE TERRINE

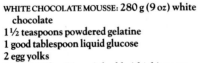

WHITE CHOCOLATE MOUSSE: 280 g (9 oz) white
   chocolate
1½ teaspoons powdered gelatine
1 good tablespoon liquid glucose
2 egg yolks
155 ml (5 fl oz/⅔ cup) double (thick) cream
155 ml (5 fl oz/⅔ cup) thick sour cream

DARK CHOCOLATE MOUSSE: 185 g (6 oz) plain (dark)
   chocolate
4 tablespoons strong black coffee
2 teaspoons powdered gelatine
125 g (4 oz/½ cup) butter, cut into cubes
2 egg yolks
315 ml (10 fl oz/1¼ cups) whipping cream

To make dark chocolate mousse, melt chocolate with coffee in the top of a double boiler or a bowl set over a pan of simmering water. Sprinkle gelatine over 3 tablespoons water in a small bowl and leave to soften for 2-3 minutes. Stand bowl in a pan of hot water and stir until gelatine has dissolved. Stir into chocolate with butter and beat until butter has melted and everything is well mixed. Leave to cool, then beat in egg yolks. In a bowl, whip cream lightly and fold into chocolate mixture.

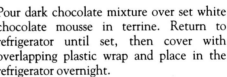

Line a 1 kg (2 lb) loaf tin with plastic wrap to overlap edges. To make the white chocolate mousse, break the white chocolate into small pieces and set aside. Sprinkle gelatine over 2 tablespoons water in a small bowl and leave to soften for 2-3 minutes. Put 3 tablespoons water in a saucepan with glucose and bring to the boil. Remove from heat and stir in gelatine until dissolved. Add chocolate and beat mixture until chocolate has melted and is smooth.

Pour dark chocolate mixture over set white chocolate mousse in terrine. Return to refrigerator until set, then cover with overlapping plastic wrap and place in the refrigerator overnight.

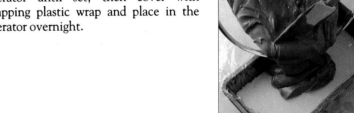

Beat in egg yolks, one at a time. In a bowl, whip the creams together lightly and fold into the chocolate mixture. Pour the chocolate into the loaf tin and refrigerate until set.

When ready to serve, unfold plastic wrap from top of mousse and turn out onto a serving dish. Carefully peel off plastic wrap and serve terrine cut in slices.

Serves 8-10.

Note: Decorate the terrine with whipped cream and grated chocolate, if desired. Either mousse can be served as a dessert on its own and will serve 4 people.

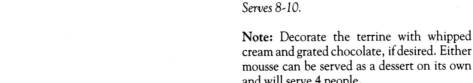

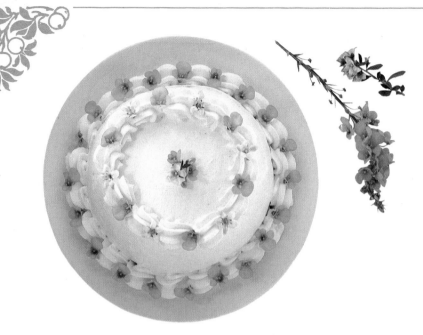

NEGRESSE EN CHEMISE

185 g (6 oz) plain (dark) chocolate
5 tablespoons strong black coffee
185 g (6 oz/¾ cup) unsalted butter
185 g (6 oz/¾ cup) caster sugar
5 large eggs, beaten
375 ml (12 fl oz/1½ cups) whipping cream

Preheat oven to 180C (350F/Gas 4). Line a 1 litre (32 fl oz/4 cup) pudding bowl or soufflé dish with double thickness of foil.

Melt chocolate with coffee in top of a double boiler or a bowl set over a saucepan of simmering water. Gradually beat in butter and sugar and heat until mixture is hot. Remove from heat and gradually whisk in eggs. Strain mixture into prepared dish, cover with foil and place in a roasting tin. Add boiling water to tin to come halfway up dish, then bake in the oven for 65 minutes, until top has a thick crust. Cool, then refrigerate.

When ready to serve, unmould pudding onto a serving dish and peel away foil – you need to do this carefully as the pudding is rich and sticky. In a bowl, whip cream stiffly, then cover the cake with two-thirds of it. Use remainder to pipe cream rosettes round top edge and base of cake.

Serves 6-8.

Note: The pudding looks very pretty decorated with tiny sprigs of fresh flowers.

RICH CHOCOLATE LOG

440 g (14 oz) can condensed milk
90 g (3 oz) plain (dark) chocolate
45 g (1½ oz/9 teaspoons) butter
500 g (1 lb) plain sponge cake
125 g (4 oz/⅔ cup) glacé cherries, halved
45 g (1½ oz/½ cup) walnuts, chopped
45 g (1½ oz/3 tablespoons) stoned dates, chopped

CHOCOLATE FUDGE ICING: 45 g (1½ oz/9 teaspoons) butter
60 g (2 oz/¼ cup) caster sugar
90 g (3 oz/½ cup) icing sugar
30 g (1 oz/¼ cup) cocoa

Put milk, chocolate and butter in a saucepan and stir over low heat until chocolate and butter have melted and ingredients are well combined. Remove from heat. Reduce cake to crumbs in a blender or food processor and stir into chocolate mixture. Stir in the cherries, walnuts and dates. Spoon mixture onto a large piece of greaseproof paper and form into a log shape. Roll up in the paper and chill overnight.

Two hours before serving, unwrap roll and place on serving dish. To make the fudge icing, melt the butter in a saucepan with caster sugar and 2 tablespoons water. Bring to boiling point. Sift icing sugar and cocoa into pan and beat well. Cool until fudgy, then spread over roll. Mark lines along roll with a fork to give a log effect.

Serves 8-10.

PINEAPPLE ALASKA

1 large ripe pineapple with leaves
1-2 tablespoons kirsch
1 litre (32 fl oz/4 cups) vanilla ice cream
3 egg whites
185 g (6 oz/¾ cup) caster sugar
1 tablespoon caster sugar for sprinkling

Cut pineapple and leafy 'plume' in half lengthwise. Using a grapefruit knife, cut out flesh. Discard core, then cut flesh into chunks and put into a bowl. Sprinkle with kirsch, cover with plastic wrap and chill overnight with pineapple shells.

Put pineapple chunks back into shells and pack ice cream on top. Put in freezer for about 2 hours, until very firm. Meanwhile, preheat oven to 200C (400F/Gas 6). Just before serving, whisk egg whites in a bowl until stiff. Whisk in half the sugar, whisking for 1 minute more. Fold in remaining sugar.

Pile this meringue over ice cream, making sure it is completely covered. Make small peaks in meringue with a flat-bladed knife. Place pineapple shells on a baking sheet and sprinkle with the 1 tablespoon caster sugar. Bake in the oven for about 8 minutes, until meringue is browned. Serve immediately.

Serves 6.

Variation: Try making this dessert using a fruit sorbet instead of ice cream.

MANGO MOUSSE

440 g (14 oz) can mangoes
juice of ½ lemon
1-2 tablespoons caster sugar
3 teaspoons powdered gelatine
315 ml (10 fl oz/1¼ cups) whipping cream
fresh mango slices and lemon peel strips, to decorate

Drain mangoes well and purée flesh with lemon juice in a blender or food processor. Pour into a bowl and sweeten to taste with caster sugar.

Sprinkle gelatine over 5 tablespoons water in a small bowl and leave to soften for 2-3 minutes. Stand bowl in a saucepan of hot water and stir until gelatine has dissolved. Stir into purée, then put in a cool place until on point of setting. In a bowl, whip cream lightly and fold into mango mixture.

Pour mixture into a glass serving bowl or individual glasses and chill until set. Decorate with fresh mango slices and lemon peel just before serving.

Serves 4.

Note: When folding whipped cream and/or egg whites into gelatine mixtures, it is essential that the base mixture is on the point of setting. If folded in too soon, the mixture will separate out to jelly on the bottom and froth on top.

ICED LOGANBERRY SOUFFLÉ

LYCHEE SORBET

500 g (1 lb) loganberries or raspberries
lemon juice, to taste
155 g (5 oz/⅔ cup) caster sugar
3 egg whites
470 ml (15 fl oz/1¾ cups) whipping cream
raspberries and mint sprigs, to decorate

Purée fruit in a blender or food processor, then sieve to remove seeds. Flavour with lemon juice.

Put sugar and 125 ml (4 fl oz/½ cup) water into a small saucepan and place on a low heat. When sugar has dissolved, bring syrup to boil and boil to soft ball stage, 115C (240F). In a large bowl, whisk egg whites until stiff. Gradually pour in sugar syrup, whisking all the time. Continue whisking until meringue is firm and cool. In a bowl, whip cream lightly and fold into meringue mixture with fruit purée.

Divide mixture between 6 ramekin dishes and freeze for 2-3 hours. Transfer to the refrigerator about 30 minutes before serving. Decorate with raspberries and mint.

Serves 6.

Note: For a special occasion, prepare small ramekin dishes by securing pieces of foil around them, to come above top of dish. Keep in place with freezer tape. Pour mixture into dishes to come over the top, so when foil removed, they look like risen soufflés.

two 440 g (14 oz) cans lychees in syrup
juice and grated peel of 1 lemon
2 egg whites
mint sprigs, to decorate

Drain lychees, reserving 315 ml (10 fl oz/1¼ cups) syrup. Purée lychees with the syrup and lemon juice in a blender or food processor.

Stir in lemon peel, tip into a plastic container and freeze for about 1 hour, until mixture is slushy and semi-frozen.

In a large bowl, whisk egg whites until stiff. Tip in semi-frozen lychee purée and fold together to combine thoroughly. Return to freezer until firm. Serve the sorbet decorated with sprigs of mint.

Serves 4-6.

Note: If time permits, whisk sorbet once more about 1 hour after adding egg whites. This gives a smoother texture. Serve sorbets soon after making for the best flavour.

TARTE FRANÇAISE

410 g (13 oz) puff pastry, thawed if frozen
1 egg yolk, beaten
6 tablespoons apricot jam, sieved
2 tablespoons lemon juice
about 750 g (1½ lb) mixed fresh fruit, such as grapes,
   strawberries and/or raspberries and bananas

Preheat oven to 220C (425F/Gas 7). Roll out pastry to a 30 x 20 cm (12 x 8 in) rectangle. Fold pastry in half, to a 15 x 20 cm (6 x 8 in) rectangle. Cut a rectangle from folded edge, 4 cm (1½ in) in from outside edges.

Unfold middle section and roll out to same size as 'frame' – 30 x 20 cm (12 x 8 in). Place on a baking sheet, dampen edges with water, then unfold 'frame' and place carefully on top of pastry rectangle. Press edges of pastry together, then 'knock up' using a blunt knife. Mark a pattern on frame and brush with beaten egg yolk. Prick centre of case all over.

Leave pastry in a cool place for 10 minutes, then bake for about 20 minutes, until golden brown. Leave to cool. Put jam and lemon juice into a saucepan and heat gently until jam has melted. To prepare fruit, halve and seed grapes, leave strawberries and/or raspberries whole and peel and slice bananas. Brush base of tart lightly with jam and arrange fruit in rows. Brush fruit with jam and serve as soon as possible.

Serves 6.

STRAWBERRY MILLE FEUILLE

410 g (13 oz) puff pastry, thawed if frozen
500 g (1 lb) fresh strawberries
315 ml (10 fl oz/1¼ cups) whipping cream
1-2 drops vanilla essence
caster sugar, to taste
5 tablespoons redcurrant jelly

Preheat oven to 220C (425F/Gas 7). Roll out the pastry to a thin rectangle and cut it into 3 even sections.

Place sections on baking sheets and prick all over with a fork. Bake in the oven for 15-20 minutes, until golden brown and crisp. Cool on a wire rack. When cold, trim edges with a very sharp knife to make even. Reserve trimmings. Cut half of the strawberries in half – choose even-sized ones for this. Slice remainder. In a bowl, whip cream fairly stiffly and flavour with vanilla essence and sugar. Fold sliced strawberries into cream.

Put a pastry slice onto a serving plate and spread with half the cream mixture. Lay another slice on top and spread with remaining cream mixture. Top with third slice. Put redcurrant jelly and 2 tablespoons water into a small saucepan and heat gently until jelly has dissolved. Brush top slice with a little jelly and arrange halved strawberries on top. Brush with remainder of jelly. Crush reserved pastry trimmings and press into sides of slice with the blade of a knife.

Serves 6-8.

VICTORIA SPONGE

125 g (4 oz/½ cup) soft tub margarine or butter,
   softened
125 g (4 oz/½ cup) caster sugar
2 large eggs
125 g (4 oz/1 cup) self-raising flour
milk, if needed

TO SERVE: whipped cream
fresh fruit

Preheat oven to 180C (350F/Gas 4). Grease
two 17.5 cm (7 in) round sandwich tins or a
20 cm (8 in) square tin.

In a bowl, cream margarine or butter and
sugar together until light and fluffy. Beat eggs
in a separate small bowl, then beat into
mixture a little at a time. Sift flour into
mixture and fold in using a metal spoon.
Mixture should be a soft dropping
consistency – add a little milk if necessary.
Spoon into prepared tin(s). Bake in the oven
for about 15 or 25 minutes, depending on tin
size, until top is golden and spongy to touch.
Turn out and cool on a wire rack.

To serve, spread whipped cream on one round
cake and arrange fruit on top. Sandwich with
other cake. Spread a square cake with
whipped cream mixed with some fruit, and
arrange remainder over top.

Serves 6.

Variations: Beat a few drops of vanilla
essence or 1 tablespoon grated orange or
lemon peel into mixture before adding flour.
Ice the cake with water icing, or flavoured
butter icing, if desired.

SPIKY COFFEE BRANDY CAKE

1 quantity of Victoria Sponge mixture (see left)
2 tablespoons brandy
3 teaspoons caster sugar
315 ml (10 fl oz/1¼ cups) hot strong black coffee
315 ml (10 fl oz/1¼ cups) whipping cream
3 teaspoons icing sugar
60 g (2 oz/½ cup) split almonds, toasted

Preheat oven to 180C (350F/Gas 4). Bake
cake in a 625 ml (20 fl oz/2½ cup) greased
pudding bowl and leave to cool in the bowl.

When cake is cold, stir brandy and caster
sugar into hot coffee and pour over cake (still
in the bowl). Put a saucer over the bowl and
refrigerate overnight.

About 2 hours before serving, run a knife
around edges of cake, then turn out onto a
serving plate. In a bowl, whip cream with
icing sugar until very stiff and spread evenly
over cake, covering completely. Refrigerate.
Immediately before serving, stick toasted
almonds into surface of cream all over cake.

Serves 4-6.

Variation: For a special occasion, pipe
rosettes of cream all over the cake, then
decorate with almonds and flowers.

CHERRY SPONGE FLANS

1 quantity of Victoria Sponge mixture (see page 88)
500 g (1 lb) fresh cherries, stoned
1 tablespoon caster sugar
1 teaspoon arrowroot
1 tablespoon kirsch
315 ml (10 fl oz/1¼ cups) whipping cream

Preheat oven to 180C (350F/Gas 4). Grease 8 individual 10 cm (4 in) Yorkshire pudding tins. Divide the sponge mixture between prepared tins and bake for 5-10 minutes, until golden and spongy to touch.

Leave in tins to cool. Put cherries into a saucepan with sugar. Cover pan and cook over low heat until juices run. Mix arrowroot to a smooth paste with 1 tablespoon water and add to cherries. Bring to boil, stirring, then remove from heat and leave to cool. Stir in kirsch.

When ready to serve, place sponges on individual serving plates. Spoon cherries in their thick sauce on top. In a bowl, whip cream stiffly and pipe a border round the cherries. Serve immediately.

Serves 8.

Note: Arrowroot is a thickening agent like cornflour, but it does not turn a sauce cloudy. It is more usually used than cornflour to thicken sweet sauces.

CHOC CHESTNUT GÂTEAU

185 g (6 oz/¾ cup) butter, softened
125 g (4 oz/½ cup) caster sugar
185 g (6 oz) plain (dark) chocolate
3 tablespoons strong black coffee
440 g (14 oz) can unsweetened chestnut purée
315 ml (10 fl oz/1¼ cups) whipping cream
marrons glacés, to decorate, if desired

Oil a loose-bottomed or springform 20 cm (8 in) round or 1 kg (2 lb) loaf tin. Cream butter and sugar in a bowl until they are light and fluffy.

Melt chocolate with coffee in top of a double boiler or bowl set over a saucepan of simmering water. Add chestnut purée to butter mixture with melted chocolate and beat until smooth. Spoon mixture into prepared tin and level surface. Cover with foil and freeze for 3 hours.

Turn out onto a serving plate. Whip cream stiffly in a bowl and pipe over top. Decorate with marrons glacés, if using. Let cake stand for 30 minutes at room temperature to soften before serving.

Serves 6-8.

Note: If butter is too hard to cream easily, add 1-2 teaspoons hot milk to it.

WALNUT GÂTEAU

HOT ORANGE CAKE

155 g (5 oz/1 cup) stoned dates, chopped
250 ml (8 fl oz/1 cup) boiling water
125 g (4 oz/½ cup) butter, softened
1 egg
220 g (7 oz/1 cup) caster sugar
few drops vanilla essence
185 g (6 oz/1½ cups) plain flour
1 teaspoon each bicarbonate of soda, baking powder
  and salt
60 g (2 oz/½ cup) walnuts, chopped

BUTTERSCOTCH ICING: 2 tablespoons whipping cream
knob of butter
2 tablespoons soft brown sugar

125 g (4 oz/½ cup) butter, softened
125 g (4 oz/½ cup) caster sugar
2 large eggs, separated
125 g (4 oz/1 cup) self-raising flour
juice and grated peel of 3 small oranges
250 ml (8 fl oz/1 cup) double (thick) cream
icing sugar
fresh orange segments

Preheat oven to 180C (350F/Gas 4). Well
grease a deep 20 cm (8 in) non-stick cake tin.
In a large bowl, cream butter and sugar until
light and fluffy. Beat egg yolks into mixture
with 1 tablespoon flour and juice and grated
peel of 1 orange.

Preheat oven to 180C (350F/Gas 4). Grease
and line a 20 cm (8 in) cake tin or 1 kg (2 lb)
loaf tin. Put dates in a bowl with boiling
water. Leave to cool. In a bowl, cream butter,
egg, sugar and vanilla essence together until
light and fluffy. Sift dry ingredients together
into mixture and fold in with the dates and
soaking liquid. Fold in chopped walnuts and
pour mixture into a prepared tin. Bake in the
oven for 1-1½ hours, until spongy to touch.
Turn out of the tin.

In a separate bowl, whisk egg whites until
stiff, but not dry. Fold into mixture with
remaining flour and spoon into the prepared
cake tin. Bake in the oven for 20-30 minutes,
until golden brown and springy to touch.

The gâteau can be served warm or cold,
covered with the icing. To make icing, put
cream, butter and brown sugar into a small
saucepan and stir over medium heat. Bring to
boil and pour over cake. Serve at once.

Serves 6-8.

Note: To prevent dates sticking when
chopping them, dip the knife in hot water.

While cake is cooking, whip cream stiffly in a
bowl with remaining orange juice and peel.
Leave cake in tin for 2-3 minutes, then turn
out and cut in half horizontally. Working
quickly, spread bottom with cream, cover
with top half. Dust thickly with icing sugar
and arrange orange segments on top. Serve
the cake at once.

Serves 6.

Note: The cream will melt into the hot cake,
so serve as quickly as possible.

RUM TRUFFLE CAKE

220 g (7 oz) plain (dark) chocolate
125 g (4 oz/½ cup) unsalted butter
75 ml (2½ fl oz/⅓ cup) dark rum
3 eggs, separated
125 g (4 oz/½ cup) caster sugar
90 g (3 oz/¾ cup) plain flour
60 g (2 oz/½ cup) ground almonds

ICING: 220 g (7 oz) plain (dark) chocolate
315 ml (10 fl oz/1¼ cups) double (thick) cream
3 teaspoons dark rum
60 g (2 oz) white chocolate, grated

Butter and flour a 20 cm (8 in) round cake tin
and line base with greaseproof paper.

Preheat oven to 180C (350F/Gas 4). Place
chocolate and butter in a bowl over a
saucepan of hand-hot water. Stir occasionally
until melted. Add rum and stir well.

Place egg yolks and sugar in a bowl over a
saucepan of simmering water. Whisk until
thick and pale, remove bowl from pan and
continue to whisk until mixture leaves a trail
when whisk is lifted. Stir in chocolate
mixture until evenly blended. Mix together
flour and ground almonds, add to mixture and
fold in carefully using a spatula.

Whisk egg whites until stiff, fold in ⅓ at a
time until all egg white has been
incorporated. Pour mixture into tin and bake
in the oven for 45-55 minutes until firm to
touch in centre. Turn out of tin and cool on a
wire rack.

To make the icing, melt 125 g (4 oz) of the
chocolate with 60 ml (2 fl oz/¼ cup) cream in
a bowl over a pan of hot water. Stir in rum
until well blended. Leave to cool. Whip 125
ml (4 fl oz/½ cup) cream in a bowl until
thick, add ½ chocolate rum mixture and fold
in to make a smooth icing.

Cut cake in half, sandwich together with the
chocolate icing and spread remainder over
top and sides. Chill cake and remaining ½ of
chocolate rum mixture until firm. Melt
remaining chocolate and cream in a bowl, stir
until smooth; cool and pour mixture over
cake to cover evenly. Shape firmed chocolate
rum mixture into 16 truffles, coat in grated
white chocolate. Arrange on top of cake;
chill to set.

Makes 10-12 slices.

GLACÉ FRUIT CAKE

315 g (10 oz) mixed glacé fruit,
  chopped
125 g (4 oz/1 cup) dried apricots, chopped
125 g (4 oz/1 cup) chopped pecan nuts
finely grated peel and juice of 1 lemon
375 g (12 oz/3 cups) plain flour
1 teaspoon baking powder
1½ teaspoons ground mixed spice
185 g (6 oz/1⅔ cups) ground almonds
375 g (12 oz/1¾ cups) caster sugar
375 g (12 oz/1½ cups) butter, softened
4 eggs

TOPPING: 60 ml (2 fl oz/¼ cup) apricot jam
mixed glacé fruit and nuts
sprig of fresh holly

Line a 20 cm (8 in) square cake tin, or a 22.5
cm (9 in) round tin, with double thickness
greased greaseproof paper. Tie a double
thickness band of brown paper around tin and
stand tin on double thickness lined baking
sheet. Preheat oven to 140C (275F/Gas 1).
Mix glacé fruit with apricots, nuts, lemon
peel and juice; stir. Sift flour, baking powder
and mixed spice into a bowl, add almonds,
sugar, butter and eggs. Mix, then beat for 2
minutes. Stir in fruit and nuts.

Put in tin; smooth top. Bake in oven for
2¼-2½ hours, or until the cake feels firm and
springy when pressed in centre. Cool in tin;
turn out and wrap in foil. Place jam and 2
teaspoons water in a pan, bring to boil,
stirring; sieve. Brush top of cake with glaze,
arrange fruit and nuts over top; brush with
remaining glaze. Leave to set, tie with
ribbon. Decorate with holly.

Makes 30 slices.

MARASCHINO FRUIT RING

125 g (4 oz/1 cup) wholemeal self-raising flour
125 g (4 oz/¾ cup) light soft brown sugar
125 g (4 oz/½ cup) butter, softened
3 eggs
90 g (3 oz/½ cup) pecan nuts, chopped
90 g (3 oz/½ cup) raisins
90 g (3 oz/½ cup) red cocktail cherries
90 g (3 oz/½ cup) green glacé cherries

DECORATION: 90 g (3 oz/½ cup) icing sugar, sieved
8 teaspoons maraschino cherry syrup
6 red and 6 green cherries, sliced

Preheat oven to 150C (300F/Gas 2). Lightly
oil a 22.5 cm (9 in) ring mould. Place flour,
sugar, butter and eggs in a mixing bowl. Stir
together until well mixed, then beat for 1-2
minutes until smooth and glossy. Add nuts,
raisins and cherries to mixture and stir until
evenly mixed. Spoon mixture into ring
mould and level top. Bake in the oven for
about 1 hour until cake feels firm to touch or
until a skewer inserted in centre comes out
clean.

Loosen edges of cake with a knife and cool in
tin. Invert onto a wire rack. To decorate, put
icing sugar in a bowl, stir in enough cherry
syrup to mix to the consistency of thick
cream. Spoon icing over cold cake, arrange
sliced cherries in clusters around top of cake.
Leave to set.

Serves 10.

KASTOBERSTORTE

4 eggs
9 teaspoons caster sugar
6 teaspoons plain flour
6 teaspoons cornflour
250 g (8 oz) medium fat curd cheese
155 ml (5 fl oz/⅔ cup) natural yogurt
60 g (2 oz/⅓ cup) raisins
finely grated peel and juice of 1 orange
155 ml (5 fl oz/⅔ cup) whipping cream
3 teaspoons powdered gelatine
6 teaspoons clear honey
icing sugar for dusting

Preheat oven to 200C (400F/Gas 6). Lightly grease 2 baking sheets and line with non-stick baking parchment. Mark two 22.5 cm (9 in) circles on baking parchment.

Using a rotary or hand-held whisk, beat 2 eggs and the sugar in a bowl until mixture is thick enough to hold trail of whisk when beaters are lifted. Sift flours over eggs and fold in with a large metal spoon.

Spoon mixture onto baking sheets, spreading it beyond circles. Bake in the oven for 12–15 minutes with oven door open 1 cm (½ in).

Meanwhile, make filling, blend cheese, yogurt, raisins and orange peel and juice in a bowl. Whip cream and fold in. Sprinkle gelatine over 2 tablespoons water in a small bowl and leave to soften for 2–3 minutes. Stand bowl in a saucepan of hot water and stir until dissolved and quite hot. Stir into cheese. Beat remaining eggs and honey until thick, then fold into cheese.

Using a sharp knife, trim sponges to 22.5 cm (9 in) diameter. Fit one sponge into a 22.5 cm (9 in) loose-bottomed cake tin. Pour filling on top and refrigerate for 2–3 hours until set. Place second sponge on filling and dust with icing sugar.

Serves 8.

TOFU BANANA CHEESECAKE

60 g (2 oz/¼ cup) butter
125 g (4 oz/1¼ cups) rich tea biscuit crumbs
FILLING:
375 g (12 oz) tofu, cut into small pieces
375 g (12 oz) cottage cheese
2 ripe bananas, chopped
3 teaspoons clear honey
3 teaspoons plain flour
finely grated peel and juice of 1 lime
TO DECORATE:
2 bananas
60 g (2 oz/¼ cup) apricot jam
3 teaspoons lemon juice
30 g (1 oz) angelica

Preheat oven to 180C (350F/Gas 4). Grease and line a 20 cm (8 in) round, loose-bottomed cake tin. In a saucepan, melt butter, then add biscuit crumbs. Mix well, then press into base of cake tin.

Put tofu into a bowl and stir in cheese, chopped bananas, honey and flour. Beat well, then stir in lime peel and juice. Spoon onto biscuit base and bake in the oven for 45 minutes.

To decorate, slice bananas diagonally into oval shapes. Arrange slices around edge of cheesecake. Put jam into a saucepan with lemon juice. Bring to the boil, then brush over the banana slices. Cut angelica into leaf shapes and arrange on banana slices.

Serves 8–10.

MARBLED CHEESECAKE

60 g (2 oz/¼ cup) butter
185 g (6 oz/1⅔ cups) digestive biscuit crumbs
FILLING:
750 g (1½ lb) medium fat soft cheese
90 g (3 oz/⅓ cup) caster sugar
3 teaspoons plain flour
3 eggs
few drops vanilla essence
90 g (3 oz) plain (dark) chocolate, broken into pieces

Preheat oven to 180C (350F/Gas 4). Grease a 20 cm (8 in) round, loose-bottomed cake tin. In a saucepan, melt butter, then stir in biscuit crumbs. Mix well, then press the mixture into base of cake tin.

In a bowl, beat cheese, sugar, flour, eggs and vanilla essence. Spoon onto biscuit base and set aside.

Melt chocolate in the top of a double boiler or a bowl set over a saucepan of simmering water. Pour melted chocolate in a thin stream over cheese mixture. Using the handle of a teaspoon, swirl the 2 mixtures to create a marbled effect.

Bake in the oven for 45 minutes. Leave cheesecake to cool before removing from the tin.

Serves 8–10.

BOSTON CHEESECAKE

90 g (3 oz/⅓ cup) butter
250 g (8 oz/2¼ cups) rich tea biscuit crumbs
¼ teaspoon ground cinnamon
¼ teaspoon ground allspice
FILLING:
500 g (1 lb) full fat soft cheese
250 ml (8 fl oz/1 cup) thick sour cream
155 g (5 oz/⅔ cup) caster sugar
4 eggs, separated
6 teaspoons plain flour
few drops vanilla essence
finely grated peel and juice of 1 lemon
TO SERVE:
icing sugar

Preheat oven to 180C (350F/Gas 4). Grease and line a 22.5 cm (9 in) round, loose-bottomed tin. In a saucepan, melt butter, then stir in biscuit crumbs and spices. Mix well, then press into base of cake tin.

In a bowl, beat cheese, sour cream, 90 g (3 oz/⅓ cup) sugar, egg yolks, flour, vanilla essence and lemon peel and juice until smooth.

Whisk egg whites in a separate bowl with remaining sugar until stiff. Fold into cheese mixture with a large metal spoon. Turn into cake tin and bake in the oven for 1 hour.

Leave to cool before removing from the tin. To decorate, cut out 5 strips of greaseproof paper 2 cm (¾ in) wide and lay them at intervals over surface of cheesecake. Sift icing sugar over the top. Carefully remove strips and serve.

Serves 10–12.

— STRAWBERRY CHEESECAKE —

90 g (3 oz/⅓ cup) butter

125 g (4 oz/1¼ cups) rich tea biscuit crumbs

FILLING:

250 g (8 oz) Ricotta cheese

155 ml (5 fl oz/⅔ cup) natural yogurt

155 ml (5 fl oz/⅔ cup) thick sour cream

2 eggs, separated

finely grated peel and juice of 1 orange

500 g (1 lb) strawberries

5 teaspoons powdered gelatine

60 g (2 oz/¼ cup) caster sugar

TO DECORATE:

155 ml (5 fl oz/⅔ cup) whipping cream

Grease and line a 22.5 cm (9 in) round, loose-bottomed cake tin. In a saucepan, melt butter, then stir in biscuit crumbs. Mix well, then press into base of cake tin.

In a bowl, beat cheese, yogurt, sour cream, egg yolks, orange peel and juice. Reserve 10 strawberries for decoration. Blend remainder in a food processor or blender for 30 seconds or until puréed. Stir into cheese mixture.

Sprinkle gelatine over 2 tablespoons water in a small bowl and leave to soften for 2–3 minutes. Stand the bowl in a saucepan of hot water and stir until dissolved and quite hot. Stir into cheese mixture.

Whisk egg whites in a bowl with sugar until firm. Fold into strawberry cheese with a large metal spoon. Turn into cake tin and leave in the refrigerator to set for 2–3 hours.

To decorate, whip cream and pipe a border of 20 rosettes around top edge of cheesecake. Halve reserved strawberries and top each rosette with a strawberry half.

Serves 8–10.

— TUTTI FRUTTI CHEESECAKE —

packet of 8 trifle sponges

FILLING:

375 g (12 oz) full fat soft cheese

60 g (2 oz/¼ cup) caster sugar

2 eggs

3 teaspoons powdered gelatine

30 g (1 oz/¼ cup) flaked almonds

30 g (1 oz/¼ cup) chopped mixed citrus peel

30 g (1 oz/¼ cup) chopped raisins

9 teaspoons Grand Marnier

30 g (1 oz/¼ cup) chopped glacé cherries

TO DECORATE:

5 glacé cherries, halved

30 g (1 oz) angelica, cut into small strips

Grease and line a 20 x 10 cm (8 x 4 in) loaf tin. To make filling, beat cheese, sugar and eggs in a bowl until light and fluffy.

Sprinkle gelatine over 2 tablespoons water in a small bowl and leave to soften for 2–3 minutes. Stand the bowl in a saucepan of hot water and stir until dissolved and quite hot. Stir into cheese mixture.

Stir in flaked almonds, mixed citrus peel, raisins, Grand Marnier and glacé cherries. Turn into cake tin.

Cut trifle sponges to fit the tin and arrange on top of the filling. Leave to set in the refrigerator for 2–3 hours.

To decorate, turn out cheesecake onto a serving dish and decorate the top with halved glacé cherries and angelica.

Serves 10.

INDEX

Anchovy Mayonnaise 77
Apple & Elderflower Pork 40
Apple & Rum Crêpes 58
Arnold Bennett Omelette 60
Avocado Crab Louis 68

Bacon Parcels 71
Banana Brûlée 79
Barbecued Trout in Leaves 30
Basic Crêpes 52
Basic Omelette 59
Beef & Pasta Soup 14
Beef in Wine 40
Beef-Stuffed Cabbage 39
Bolognese Crêpes 55
Boston Cheesecake 94
Bouillabaisse 16
Breakfast Omelette 62
Buttered Herb Sole Fillets 30

Caribbean Crêpes 56
Celeriac & Mussels 66
Charlotte Russe 80
Cheesy Anchovy Crêpes 52
Cheesy Meatball Fondue 73
Cherry & Almond Layer 56
Cherry Sponge Flans 89
Chicken Bites 47
Chicken Liver Omelette 61
Chicken Noodle Soup 12
Chicken Satay 21
Choc Chestnut Gâteau 89
Chocolate Trifle 82
Christmas Omelette 65
Clementine Duck 38
Coconut Spiced Cod 34
Coeurs à la Crème 78
Coffee Bombe 80
Cool Avocado Dip 77
Coronation Chicken 69
Coulibiac 28
Country Mushroom Soup 9
Crab & Sweetcorn Soup 8
Cranberry & Orange Duck 49
Cream of Asparagus Soup 17
Crispy Grapefruit Chicken 47
Crispy Sausage Bites 74
Cucumber Yogurt Sauce 77
Curried Chicken Crêpes 54
Curried Drumsticks 48

Devilled Turkey Wings 48
Dijon Surprise Omelette 65

Egg Foo Yung 63

Fish & Pasta Pie 29
Fish Crespolini 53
Fish Pâté 22
Fondue Accompaniments 77
Fondue Bourguignonne 71
Framboise Zabaglione 82
French Chestnut Crêpes 57
French Country Cod Steaks 31
French Onion Soup 11
Fruit Pork Pillows 37
Fruity Duck Fondue 73

Gammon Steaks 42
German Sausage Salad 70
Glacé Fruit Cake 92
Golden Turkey 49
Gooseberry Goose 36
Goulash Soup 14
Grand Marnier Pâté 23
Grilled Florida Cocktail 25
Grilled Prawns 19

Ham & Herb Omelette 62
Herb & Garlic Mussels 18
Herb Baked Eggs 26
Horseradish Sauce 77
Horseradish Steak 41
Hot Orange Cake 90

Ice Cream Crêpes 58
Iced Loganberry Soufflé 86
Indonesian Seafood Salad 67
Italian Bean & Pasta Soup 10
Italian Pizza Omelette 64

Juniper Lamb 41

Kastoberstorte 93
Kedgeree 28
Kipper Salad 67

Lamb & Noodle Squash 68
Lobster Bisque 16
Lychee Sorbet 86

Madras Curried Crabs 34
Mange Tout Soup 15
Mango Mousse 85
Maraschino Fruit Ring 92
Marbled Cheesecake 94
Mexican Fondue 75
Middle Eastern Fondue 75
Minced Lamb Fondue 74
Mixed Chocolate Terrine 83
Mulligatawny 13
Mussels with Basil Sauce 31
Mustard Sauce 77

Negresse en Chemise 84
New England Clam Chowder 7

Oeufs à la Neige 81
Orange Caramel Cream 78
Orange Glaze 23
Orange Liqueur Gâteau 57
Oriental Chicken Salad 69
Oriental Chicken Soup 13

Parma Ham Roulades 21
Parma Ham with Figs 24
Peppercorn Steaks 42
Peppered Pork 43
Pheasant in Madeira 50
Pineapple Alaska 85
Pink Trout Salad 70
Pipérade 64
Ploughman's Soup 10
Pomegranate & Lime Lamb 43
Potage Crème de Fromage 9
Pork Satay 76
Pork with Herbs 44
Potted Salmon 22
Poussin Provençal 51
Prawn & Tuna Crêpes 54
Prawn Barquettes 27
Prawn Soufflé Omelette 60
Provençal Fish Chowder 7
Pumpkin Soup 15

Red Berry Soufflé 81
Rich Chocolate Log 84
Rich Country Chicken Soup 12
Roast Stuffed Turkey 35
Rosy Roasted Gammon 44
Rum Truffle Cake 91

Saffron Lamb Cutlets 45
Salmon Baked Eggs 24
Salmon in Filo Pastry 32
Salmon Mousse 20
Salmon Supreme Crêpes 53
Sausage-Stuffed Mushrooms 26
Seafood Kebabs 32
Seafood Pâté 18
Shrimp Bisque 8
Smoked Fish Lasagne 29
Smoked Salmon & Dill Soup 17
Smoked Salmon Omelettes 59
Spanish Omelette 63
Spanish Prawns 19
Spiced Gammon 45
Spiced Honey Gammon 36
Spiced Skewered Lamb 46
Spicy Chicken Fondue 72
Spicy Oriental Sauce 77
Spicy Scallops 33
Spiky Coffee Brandy Cake 88
Strawberry Cheesecake 95
Strawberry Mille Feuille 87
Strudel Triangles 27
Stuffed Quail in Port 51
Stuffed Tomato Salad 66
Sweet & Sour Crêpes 55
Sweet & Sour Spare Ribs 46

Tangerine Syllabub 79
Taramasalata 20
Tarte Française 87
Teriyaki Fondue 76
Tofu Banana Cheesecake 93
Tomato & Orange Soup 11
Tortilla Loaves 61
Trout in Aspic 33
Trout Quenelles 25
Turkey Risotto 38
Turkey Stroganoff 50
Turkey Vegetable Strudel 37
Tutti Frutti Cheesecake 95

Veal Milanese 72
Victoria Sponge 88

Walnut Gâteau 90